The Secular Saints

The Secular Saints

And Why Morals Are Not Just Subjective

Hunter Lewis

Axios Press
PO Box 457
Edinburg, VA 22824
888.542.9467   info@axiosinstitute.org

Library of Congress Cataloging-in-Publication Data

Names: Lewis, Hunter, author.
Title: The secular saints : and why morals are not just subjective / Hunter
    Lewis.
Description: Edinburg, VA : Axios Press, 2018. | Includes bibliographical
    references and index.
Identifiers: LCCN 2017035727 (print) | LCCN 2017047662 (ebook) | ISBN
    9781604191196 (ebook) | ISBN 9781604191189 (hardcover)
Subjects: LCSH: Ethics--History. | Ethicists.
Classification: LCC BJ71 (ebook) | LCC BJ71 .L49 2018 (print) | DDC
    170.9--dc23
LC record available at https://lccn.loc.gov/2017035727

Contents

Part Four: Modern Moral Thinkers and Doers

Part Five: Conclusion

Part One

Introduction*

---

* This introduction includes some material first published in Hunter
Lewis, *A Question of Values: Six Ways We Make the Personal Choices
That Shape Our Lives* (San Francisco: Harper Collins, 1990).

Chapter 1

Are Morals Subjective?

WE ALL NEED food and water and shelter. But we also need to know where and how to direct our energies. We cannot function otherwise. And we need to believe we are making meaningful, not just random choices. This need is so paramount that individuals without answers will embrace anything, even the utter nihilism of terrorism, to fill the vacuum.

Religion has always helped provide answers to these questions and presumably always will. But even thousands of years ago, Greeks and Indians in particular were wondering what kind of answers, if any, could be found outside religion. If the answers come from outside revealed religion, they would have to come from our own heads. And since our brains function through some combination of emotion, intuition, sense experience, and logic, the answers would presumably have to come from those sources.

We all rely heavily on emotion to energize us, physically and mentally, but we also mistrust emotion. We know well enough that what we feel at this moment may not last long. Intuition is the mental mode we rely on the most for deciding and choosing, but it has the disadvantage of being so incommunicable to others.

In this day and age, we like factual observation and logic, and we especially like experimental science, which combines the two, because they make it so much easier to explain a conclusion to others. Isaac Newton, the great scientist, once told a colleague that something was true. When the colleague asked how he knew, Newton responded that he simply knew, but that given a day or two, he would be able to translate his knowledge into the language of fact and logic. And within a few days, he had his proof.

Given this background, it is natural for people to wonder if they might not be able to sort out moral, ethical, and related philosophical questions through some combination of intuition, fact, and logic, with the result that others would be able to understand and even accept their conclusions, without having to rely on religion and in particular revealed religion at all.

There have been many, many such attempts. Some of them were undertaken by people described in this book. That is not to say that everyone described in this book was trying to substitute human thought for religion or opposed religion in any way. Some of the people described in this book were atheists; others were devoted to their own version of religion; at least one was a very devoted Christian. Most were professional philosophers, but not all. Whatever their differences, none of them followed a religious vocation per se. They lived lives outside of organized religion, that is, they lived what might be called secular lives, whatever the religious linkages, and their thoughts and lives should be of potential interest to believers and nonbelievers alike.

But, returning to the central question, is it possible to establish a credible moral, ethical, philosophical system outside of religion? And, if so, what would it look like?

We might start to try to answer this question by pulling out some heavy ammunition from the great 18th-century British philosopher David Hume (1711–1776). Here are some particularly famous passages of his:

> If we take in our hand any volume; of divinity or school metaphysics, for instance; let us ask, Does it contain an abstract reasoning concerning quantity or number? No. Does it contain any experimental reasoning concerning matter of fact and existence? No. Commit it then to the flames:

A hundred years ago, the subjectivists were not anticipating this future. They were feeling a sense of liberation. In throwing off Church and the strictures of their Victorian forebears, they thought they were pumping fresh air into a stuffy world and claiming new ground for personal liberty. They shrugged off charges that the new liberty was really a new libertinism—so what if it were?

A Few Leading Subjectivists

The philosophers who led the attack on traditional moral philosophy and its claims for objective truth were centered in Britain and included Ludwig Wittgenstein (1889–1951, Austrian, but taught in England and wrote, in part, in English), Bertrand Russell (1872–1970), Alfred J. Ayer (1910–1989), and the American Charles Stevenson (1908–1979). They had all been taught in academic cloisters where civilized people were assumed to agree on the basics. Since the basics were a given, moral philosophy could concentrate on such hot topics as: Should one shout in public to awaken a fainted man? Slow one's car at a major intersection while carrying an injured passenger to a hospital? Or return a borrowed book on time if its continuing possession might accomplish a useful purpose?

The quartet mentioned above sought to blow all of this away, along with just about all previous philosophical thought, by arguing that ideas like free will, human nature, human ethics, beauty, and justice (moral ideas) were all equally meaningless. They were neither propositions that could be tested mathematically nor facts that could be verified by observation or experiment. They could not pass Hume's test.

A few of the more fire-breathing subjectivists took the rather paradoxical view that non-propositions and non-facts masquerading as propositions and facts were dangerous, and that both theology and moral philosophy were therefore inherently wicked. Others, such as the young Alfred J. Ayer, simply dismissed religion and moral philosophy as contentless, not much different than the barking of dogs. As Ayer wrote:

> If a sentence makes no statement at all, there is obviously no sense in asking whether what it says is either true or false. . . . To say that God exists is to make a metaphysical utterance which cannot be either true or false. . . . As we have seen, sentences which simply express moral judgments do not say anything.[1]

As time passed and the fury dissipated, subjectivists became more thoughtful about their position. Russell replied to a newspaper attack by stating:

> What Mr. X says in criticism of my views on ethics has my entire sympathy. I find my own views argumentatively irrefutable, but nevertheless incredible. . . . [The chief ground for

> adopting my view] is the complete impossi-
> bility of finding any arguments to prove that
> this or that has intrinsic value. . . . We cannot
> prove, to a color-blind man, that grass is green
> and not red. But there are various ways of prov-
> ing to him that he lacks a power of discrimi-
> nation which most men possess, whereas in
> the case of values there are no such ways. . . .
> Since no way can be even imagined for decid-
> ing a difference as to values, the conclusion
> is forced upon us that the difference is one
> of taste, not one as to any objective truth.[2]

Once he reached this position, Russell never abandoned it. But he did try to correct the more extreme
and less defensible versions of subjectivism. For example, the idea that people's moral positions are totally
contentless, just so much bubbala-bubbala, cannot be
right. When one person speaks to another about morals, communication obviously takes place, even if it is
only that, as Russell ironically put it, "ethics is the art
of recommending to others what they must do to get
along with ourselves." Picking up this clue, Charles
Stevenson found that quite a lot was going on in moral
discourse, namely, persuasion, command, grading, the
adjustment of material and other interests:

> People from widely separated communi-
> ties have different moral attitudes. Why?

To a great extent because they have been subject to different social influences. Now clearly this influence doesn't operate through sticks and stones alone; words play a great part. People praise one another, to encourage certain inclinations, and blame one another, to discourage others. Those of forceful personalities issue commands which weaker people, for complicated instinctive reasons, find it difficult to disobey, quite apart from fears of consequence. . . . Social influence is exerted, to an enormous extent, by means that have nothing to do with physical force or material reward. The ethical terms facilitate such influence. Being suited to use in suggestion, they are a means by which men's attitudes may be led this way or that.[3]

Stevenson's linguistic analysis sounds both Freudian (nothing is what it seems or seems what it is) and Marxist (arguments about good and bad are often disguised power struggles), but his conclusions are careful, prudent, and even somewhat reassuring: "good" cannot be defined; it is neither logically demonstrable nor scientifically verifiable. On the other hand, "this is good" means "I like this," and the statement "I like this" is neither contentless nor meaningless. So, human beings are not mere canine barkers.

Russell was also at pains to point out the limits of subjectivism. Although a major ethical argument cannot be settled by logic or experimental demonstration, most apparent ethical arguments are really something else. Imagine, for example, that someone proposed to eliminate all pollution control standards in the United States. The proposer would almost certainly try to bolster such a position both by reference to a variety of moral arguments ("Pollution controls are incompatible with personal liberties and incompatible with property rights.") and by reference to a variety of alleged facts ("Pollution control is expensive and reduces productivity.").

Because a variety of moral arguments and facts are used, clarity, consistency, and accuracy can all be checked.

Consequently, it would be incorrect to say that one person's position on pollution control is as good as another's. One position may be either clearer, more consistent, or more factually accurate, and if so, it is the logically superior position.

Russell concludes his defense of subjectivism with an ad hominem argument. Since ad hominem arguments are by definition illogical, this rather spoils the argument as argument. He claims that those individuals who cannot live without moral objectivity and certainty, like those who cannot live without God or God's heaven, are simply cowards:

Where traditional beliefs about the universe are concerned, craven fears ... are considered praiseworthy, while intellectual courage, unlike courage in battle, is regarded as unfeeling and materialistic.... The universe is unjust ... the secret of happiness is to face the fact that the world is horrible, horrible, horrible ... you must feel it deeply and not brush it aside. You must feel it [in your heart] and then you can start being happy again.... I cannot believe [that any good can come from] systems of thought which have their root in unworthy fears.... It is not by delusion, however exalted, that mankind can prosper, but only by unswerving courage in the pursuit of truth.[4]

It might have been entirely logical for moral philosophers, after fully embracing subjectivism, to close up shop, but there were still questions to be addressed without resorting to whether to shout at a fainted man, and as usual there was no shortage of brilliant minds attracted to the field.

Intuitionism/Utilitarianism (Derek Parfit)

In his *Reasons and Persons* (1983), Derek Parfit (1942–2017) of Oxford University combined elements of both attitudes in an engagingly eccentric effort to rescue objective ethics. Surprisingly, he begins as a thoroughgoing mystic:

> Contrary to commonsense beliefs, we are not really individuals; our selfhood, our sense of personal identity, are illusory; all of reality is one; we are elements of the whole. As Parfit comments: "The truth is very different from what we are inclined to believe.... Is the truth depressing? Some may find it so. But I find it liberating and consoling.[5]

Why is it consoling? Partly because "I care less about my death," but also because (and here we have a Benthamite twist) the absence of self kicks the stilts out from under selfishness. How can anyone want to be selfish when the self does not exist?

Although Parfit thinks he has some of the answers, there is much more work to be done:

> Belief in God, or in many gods, prevented the free development of moral reasoning. Disbelief in God, openly admitted by a majority,

is a very recent event, not yet completed. . . .
Non-Religious Ethics . . . is at a very early
stage. We cannot yet predict whether, as in
Mathematics, we will all reach agreement.
Since we cannot know how Ethics will de-
velop, it is not irrational to have high hopes.[6]

An example of the kind of logical problem that Parfit
wishes to work on:

Compare three outcomes:

> a. Peace.
>
> b. A nuclear war that kills 99 percent of the
> world's existing population.
>
> c. A nuclear war that kills 100 percent.

(B) would be worse than (a), and (c) would
be worse than (b). Which is the greater of
these two differences?

A more vexing problem is how to justify a
concern for future generations in a world
where individuals do not exist. If all reality is
one, why would a nuclear explosion matter?

Parfit disarmingly responds:

Since I failed to find the principle to which
we should appeal, I cannot explain the ob-
jection. . . . I believe that, though I have so

far failed, I or others could find the needed
principle: Theory X. But until this happens,
[it] is . . . disturbing.[7]

Parfit then displays another Benthamite twist (moral
consequences matter more than rules):

If possible [any conclusion about the im-
materiality of nuclear explosions] should
be concealed from those who will decide
whether we increase our use of nuclear energy. These people know that the Risky Policy might cause catastrophes in the further
future. It would be better if these people
believe, falsely, that the choice of the Risky
Policy would be against the interests of the
people killed by such a catastrophe. If they
have this false belief, [false because "self"
and "self-interest" have already been demonstrated to be non-existent], they would
be more likely to reach the right decision.

Finally, in a characteristic aside, Parfit concludes that:

If I or others soon solve these . . . problems,
[they] will be, in a trivial way, welcome. We
enjoy solving problems [even though with]
unsolved problems, we are further away
from the Unified Theory . . . that resolves
our disagreements [in] truth.[8]

Logical/Emotive Jacobinism

This approach suggests, once again, that moral philosophy has rested on a mistake. Traditional moral philosophers have tended to focus on the individual, as if each individual were autonomous in his or her actions. As the ancient Greeks always emphasized, however, we are social creatures, and our moral decisions are made in a specific social and political context. Even if one accepts the philosophical idea of subjectivity, therefore, it does not mean that people are free to do as they please. Quite apart from the constraint of law, there is the necessity of getting along with others. In this sense, moral subjectivity is a pseudo problem that merely clouds the real problem of social and political justice.

In one version of this argument, we construct a rational moral and political philosophy by asking ourselves what we would do if we were shipwrecked on a desert island with everyone else living on earth. What kind of "social contract" would we devise, basically starting from scratch, and not knowing the kind of society that would eventually evolve on the island? For John Rawls (1921–2002) of Harvard, the answer is that we would start with a doctrine of "fairness," that is, that

> all social values—liberty and opportunity, income and wealth, and the bases of self-respect—are to be distributed equally unless

can certainly state a fact, such as, "The watch does not work," and then derive an ought, such as, "I ought to fix the watch or throw it away." Although philosophers have usually distinguished between a watch and a human on the ground that the function of the watch is clear whereas that of a human is not, this distinction is actually quite wrong. Human purpose and function are clear: to discern what they are, one need only consult history or, as a shortcut, Aristotle's *Nichomachean Ethics*.

What, then, does Aristotle say about this? It is covered in a chapter of this book. But in MacIntyre's reading, he says that humans are social and political creatures, that their proper function and all their happiness lie in shared activity, and especially in selflessly building and serving a community. Moreover, specific virtues facilitate, but are also intrinsic to, this enterprise: honesty, fairness, reliability, consistency, obedience to law, courage, courtesy, and judgment, among others. These virtues make it possible to work together; to create friendships based not solely on the shifting sands of affection but on the surer foundation of partnership and shared accomplishment.

An individual human being, especially an individual obsessed with his or her own pleasure and well-being, is not functional and usually miserable. But a human being as a politikon zoon, a member of a family and a larger political community, can achieve "merit," "honor," "harmony," and purposefulness.

MacIntyre has no illusions that we can return to the life of a Greek city-state. Nor is he a slavish follower of Aristotle. He notes that his favorite philosopher, like all philosophers, was connected to a specific time and place—one that denigrated women and permitted slavery, among other evils—and that he paradoxically contributed to the destruction of the city-state system by serving the Macedonian tyrant Philip and by teaching Philip's son, Alexander the Great. But however difficult it might be to restore the Greek ideal derived from the city-state, what MacIntyre calls "liberal individualism" must still be firmly resisted:

> What matters at this stage is the construction of local forms of community within which civility and the intellectual and moral life can be sustained through the new dark ages which are already upon us.

Unlike most contemporary philosophers, MacIntyre has acquired a popular following. Perhaps this is because he has sought to de emphasize technique and return to the fundamental moral issues that trouble people. He has observed that studying "the concepts of morality merely by reflecting, Oxford armchair style, on what he or she or those around him or her say and do is barren" and has added that "the ideal of proof is . . . relatively barren" as well.

Muted "Moral Realists": Philippa Foot, Martha Nussbaum, and Sissela Bok

Some other philosophers, in perhaps sharpest contrast to Derek Parfit, have tried to rescue objective ethics by following Bertrand Russell's lead in reducing what we should expect from it. For example, British philosopher Philippa Foot (1920–2010) argued that we should be able to demonstrate logically that Naziism, and especially the way it treated Jews, is not a reasonable choice. But let's not expect to resolve all or even most issues this way. Some issues, especially esthetic ones, are indeed subjectively determined, and what one society believes may be unique to it but just as reasonable as what another society believes.

Foot's ideas evolved over time. Her 1958 publications "Moral Arguments" and "Moral Beliefs" sought to regain objectivist ground against the then prevalent emotivism and subjectivism. She then seemed to reconsider a bit, before again finding new ground for at least a subdued objectivism in her 2001 book *Natural Goodness*. Foot is always balanced, thoughtful, interested not just in bold outlines, but in detail and nuance.

Her most famous contribution to philosophical literature was the "trolley problem." A trolley is rapidly advancing down a track. By throwing a switch, five lives can be saved but, as a consequence, one other person will be killed. What to do? It does seem a rather artificial exercise, but in Foot's defense, people do commonly make such decisions in times of emergency, such as wartime, or even in everyday contexts such as the development of medical drugs. If a drug will help some but injure a smaller number, should be it be approved?

The difference, and it is a very important difference, between such a dilemma and the trolley problem is that when people approve drugs, they only know what might happen, not what absolutely will happen. Life at best provides probabilities, not certainties. If the question is reframed to say that by throwing the switch, five will certainly be saved, but one might be lost, it takes on quite a different character than knowing for certain that one will be lost.

Martha Nussbaum (b. 1947) agrees that ethics can be objective, to a degree. A polymath noted for contributions to many fields, among them classics, where, like Alasdair McIntyre, she is deeply influenced by Aristotle, Nussbaum thinks that there is such a thing as human nature, that it is discernible, and that it provides a foundation for reasoning about what is good for us and what is not. From this, it is an obvious step to affirm a series of virtues beginning with the foundational Aristotelian virtue of moderation.

Other moral philosophers, such as Sissela Bok (b. 1934), have also sought to develop a more sturdily objective moral philosophy by erecting it on a smaller and more modest foundation. Bok has, in particular, worked on questions of professional ethics such as those associated with medicine.

Are Ethics, Then, Subjective or Objective?

Herbert Stein, a distinguished economist, commented about a 1983 book by Paul Menzel on medical ethics:

> I repeatedly had the feeling that the only possible answers to the questions he raises [e.g., Should funds be allocated to preventative medicine or treatment? To rare killer diseases or more common, milder ones? To prolong the life of the old, or to save the young?] are: "I like it." or "I don't like it."

Is Stein correct? Has any philosopher, living or dead, really answered moral or ethical questions convincingly, or are we still stuck in the same Humean skepticism and subjectivism?

The answer to this question presented in this book, both by argument and by recording the lives and thoughts of many great thinkers and human beings, is that, in the first place, there is no such thing as Humean skepticism and subjectivism. Hume is almost always misrepresented, whether through a failure to read him carefully or a willful desire to enlist him as a friendly partisan.

The later Hume rebutted the early Hume quite convincingly. Why is this so little known? Why is Hume's skepticism forever quoted while his own answer to it is almost never quoted? The answer appears to be that the younger Hume's passionate attack on our ability to form moral judgments was written in concise, colorful, indeed unforgettable language. By contrast, the more elaborate and measured efforts of the older Hume to re-establish a way to arrive at moral and social truth is never drawn together into a few bold sentences, much less with quotable concision or rhetorical passion, so that it has to be dug out and assembled by the patient reader.

In this book, we will dig it out. Most of this is done in the chapter on Hume the moral philosopher, but we can at least have a glimpse of it here.

Hume is sometimes presented as a skeptic, sometimes as an emotivist who thought that moral or ethical judgments just reflected our emotions. He was neither. He thought, quite reasonably, that we had to integrate all our mental modes, including emotion, intuition (not to be confused with emotion), empiricism (evaluation of experience), and logic into one coherent whole in order to arrive at sensible moral or ethical judgments.

The judgments we arrive at through this integrated approach will never be certainties; they will always be probabilities. But they can reflect a high degree of probability. This is an absolutely critical point. Such judgments are always better and more reliable than our initial, unconsidered reactions. Importantly, they consider the long term, not just the short term, which the untrained human mind tends to dwell on exclusively. They put us on a sustainable path that will give us the most we can get out of life.

Very importantly, these judgments can be shared with others. They can and should be subjected to scrutiny and correction. There are answers that, if not 100% correct at all times, are generally correct. We can and should formulate them into rules that we can pass down to our children. We need such rules and cannot operate without them.

So can we derive an "ought" from an "is?" Well, not merely from an "is," which stands for our experience of the facts of the world. To get to an "ought," we need intuition and logic and emotion as well. But if we approach the problem as grown-ups, and keep our eyes clearly fixed on the long-, as well as the short-term, Hume's answer is positive. We can reach a conclusion backed by reason about what how we ought to live and what we ought to do.

Can Hume's answer be improved on? Yes. The chapter on Ludwig von Mises discusses how he clarified many points and generally improved on Hume's approach. Mises was not a moral philosopher but rather an economist. He did not address moral philosophy per se. Nor was he just a disciple of Hume, who had been both a moral philosopher and an economist. In particular, Mises put more emphasis on logic and less on experience than Hume. And his penetrating logical mind made it all much clearer.

In essence, Mises argued that our choices are always necessarily subjective, but they are made within a shared framework of reality that is quite objective. If we try to disregard this objective reality, or the rules that it imposes on us, then we will simply destroy ourselves. In this sense, the choices we face are primarily objective and therefore universal.

Mises's disciple Henry Hazlitt, in his book *The Foundations of Morality*, developed both Hume's and Mises's insights into a complete system of morality that he called cooperatism or, alternatively, mutualism. More will be said about it later.

The overarching theme of searching for moral and ethical answers will run through all the chapters of this book. But the secular saints (or at least a few of them) are worth reading for other reasons. The ideas should stimulate and challenge the reader, especially those drawn to this kind of inquiry. Some of the lives are fascinating in themselves, such as that of Jane Addams. Some people, such as Edna Lewis, teach us how to live without ever writing a word of what would generally be described as philosophy. People find so many different ways to live and express themselves, and these people's choices are as interesting as their reflections.

In closing, it should perhaps be noted that this book does not purport to offer a history of moral philosophy or even a representative sampling of important moral philosophers. Many important moral philosophers of the past were anything but secular saints. No matter what definition of secular saint is proposed, they cannot possibly fit.

One thinks of Machiavelli or Nietzsche in this regard. Both are very readable and offer important moral insights, but were rather the opposite of saints in both their doctrines and their personal lives. Others, such as the ancient Romans Cicero and Seneca, could be inspiring as well as discerning, and wise about morals and ethics, but were far too worldly or too inconsistent in their personal lives to qualify among our "saints."

Both Cicero and Seneca achieved great wealth as well as fame (Seneca was the richest man of his day apart from the Emperor Nero) and both died a bloody death, Seneca by order of Nero and Cicero by order of Marc Antony. Even so, these players at the highest and most dangerous levels of Roman power politics had an immense influence among the Christian saints of the early and later Church, and Cicero's notable work on moral philosophy, *On Duties*, considerably influenced David Hume.

The question of who is secular or who is a saint may become somewhat complicated, even if the terms are strictly defined. Plutarch was a very important and very wise ancient Greek moral philosopher and moral historian. As someone who held the post of priest of Apollo at Delphi, he would not seem to be a good example of a secular thinker. On the other hand, he may have held the post simply as a comfortable sinecure. He described the pagan religion of his time as "pleasant" and useful for ordinary people, and by saying so implied that he himself was not necessarily a "believer."

Whatever his personal beliefs, Plutarch clearly thought that atheism was dangerous, if only because people recoiled from it into superstition, and he regarded superstition as utterly poisonous to human life. In his famous "Essay on Superstition," he wrote:

> The superstitious man, if even the slightest ill befalls him, sits down and proceeds to construct, on the basis of his trouble, a fabric of harsh, momentous, and practically unavoidable experiences which he must undergo, and he also loads himself with fears and frights, suspicions and trepidations, and all this he bitterly assails with every sort of lamentation and moaning. . . .

[By contrast,] the atheist, when he is ill, takes into account and calls to mind the times when he has eaten too much or drunk too much wine, also irregularities in his daily life, or instances of over-fatigue or unaccustomed changes of air or locality; and again when he has given offence in administering office, and has encountered disrepute with the masses or calumny with a ruler, he looks to find the reason in himself and his own surroundings. . . . But in the estimation of the superstitious man, every indisposition of his body, loss of property, deaths of children, or mishaps and failures in public life are classed as "afflictions of God" or "attacks of an evil spirit . . ."

. . . There is no infirmity comprehending such a multitude of errors and emotions, and involving opinions so contradictory, or rather antagonistic, as that of superstition. We must try, therefore, to escape it in some way which is both safe and expedient, and not be like people who incautiously and blindly run hither and thither to escape from an attack of robbers or wild beasts, or from a fire, and rush into trackless places that contain pitfalls and precipices.

For thus it is that some persons, in trying to escape superstition, rush into a rough and hardened atheism, thus overleaping true religion which lies between.[10]

Although we have had to exclude many important moral philosophers in this book, some of them personal favorites, such as Plutarch, the remaining figures are not in any sense alike. They teach or inspire, or both, but in many different ways. Through their ideas, we come to understand better the choices before us and, through their training, we are better equipped to face reality and make better decisions for ourselves.

Part Two

Ancient Moral Thinkers

Chapter 2

Socrates

(469–399 BCE)

THIS CHAPTER MIGHT just as accurately have been titled Plato rather than Socrates. Our record of what Socrates is alleged to have said comes from only two principal sources: Plato's dialogues and Xenophon's *Memorabilia*. Socrates himself wrote nothing down. He spoke extemporaneously and his remarks were not recorded, so far as we can tell, on the spot, but only much later from memory.

To make matters more complicated, there is the famous Socratic Method. Socrates thought the most important lesson he could teach was how to think. He therefore usually taught by asking questions designed to bring out the reasoning of his interlocutor. The flaw in this otherwise admirable approach was that we often never learn, or cannot be sure we have discerned, Socrates's own views.

The constant process of questioning and uncovering logical lapses would also no doubt have been annoying to some of Socrates's more self-satisfied contemporaries. If so, it might have contributed to the charges against him, that he was undermining the official religion among youth, which led to his condemnation and death. In *The Apology*, Plato's account of the trial and death, Socrates candidly acknowledged:

> I go about testing and examining every man whom I think wise, whether he be a citizen or a stranger, as God has commanded me; and whenever I find that he is not wise, I point out to him on the part of God that he is not wise.

This does seem to be a formula for offending powerful people.

It seems a reasonable guess that Socrates did say this, or something like it. What motive would Plato have had for fabricating such a sincere but also endearingly naïve sentiment? Socrates also makes a great many direct statements in Plato's later dialogue, *The Republic*, unlike in some of the earlier dialogues specifically about him, when the Socratic Method so often veils his view. As a result, *The Republic* is often quoted in this short collection of Socratic sayings. But because it is a later dialogue, and less specifically about Socrates, it is reasonable to wonder whether the views expressed are truly those of Socrates, or rather Plato's much later interpretation or even modification of them. Unfortunately, there is no way to know. Like the Gospel accounts of Jesus' sayings, which were written down long after his death, they are all we have of Socrates, and we must take them as we find them.

The combined wisdom of Socrates (469–399 BCE) and Plato (428–347 BCE) comes to us from a very long time ago. In the context of their time, they are startlingly original. There is nothing like them except, to a degree, in the contemporaneous and very advanced civilization of India. It is not surprising that they have had such an immense influence on human thought.

It is also something of a miracle that we have them at all. Plato is believed to have written philosophical treatises that he considered his main life's work. But they are all gone. What remains are the dialogues, which may have been meant for the general educated public rather than other philosophers and are therefore written in a more popular style.

Here are a few sayings of Socrates to whet the reader's appetite.

The Central Role of Logic

Whenever a person strives, by the help of logic and dialectics, to start in pursuit of reality by a simple process of reason, independent of all sensory information—never flinching, until by an act of the pure intelligence, he has grasped the real nature of good—he arrives at the very end of the intellectual journey. . . . Unless he does . . . this, . . . he dreams and sleeps away his . . . life.

Plato, *The Republic*

The Nature of Dialectic

Is it the case that everything, which has an opposite, is generated only out of its opposite? . . . In fact, is it not a universal law, even though we do not always express it in so many words, that opposites are generated always out of one another, and that there is a process of generation out of one into the other?

Plato, *Phædo*

Evils, Theodorus, can never perish; for there must always remain something which is opposite to good.

Plato, *Theætetus*

Logic, Not Sense Experience, Is the Teacher

And will not a man attain to this pure thought
most completely, if he goes to each thing,
as far as he can, with his mind alone, taking neither sight nor any other sense along
with his reason in the process of thought,
to be an encumbrance?

Plato, *Phædo*

The Universe Is Itself Governed by Logic

Shall we say that the power of an irrational
principle governs all things, and that, which
is called the universe, at random, and as may
happen? Or, on the contrary, ... that Mind,
and a certain wonderful Intellect, arranges
things together, and governs throughout?

Plato, *Philebus*

The Fatal Lure of Vanity

If I were to claim to be at all wiser than others, it would be because I do not think that
I have any clear knowledge about the world,
when, in fact, I have none.

Plato, *The Apology*

What Is Truly Valuable

Athenians, I hold you in the highest regard and love; but I will obey God rather than you; and as long as I have breath and strength, I will not cease from philosophy and from exhorting you, and declaring: are you not ashamed of caring so much for the making of money, and for reputation, and for honor? Will you not think or care about wisdom, and truth, and the perfection of your soul?

Plato, *The Apology*

The Soul, Not the Body

The soul is most like the divine, the immortal, the intelligible, the uniform, the indissoluble and the unchangeable; while the body is most like the human, the mortal, the unintelligible, the multiform, the dissoluble, and the changeable.

Plato, *Phædo*

It seems that there is a narrow path which will bring us safely to our journey's end, with reason as our guide. As long as we have this body, and an evil of that sort is mingled with our souls, we shall never fully gain what we desire, which is truth. For the body is forever taking up our time with the care which it needs; and, besides whenever diseases attack it, they hinder us in our pursuit of real being. It fills us with passions, desires and fears, and all manner of phantoms, and much foolishness; and so, as the saying goes, in very truth we can never think at all for it.... While we live, we shall come nearest to knowledge, if we have no communion or intercourse with the body beyond what is absolutely necessary, and if we are not defiled with its nature. We must live pure from it until God himself releases us.

Plato, *Phædo*

But Neither Is the Body to Be Neglected or Shown Disrespect

He earnestly recommended those who conversed with him to take care of their health, both by learning whatever they could respecting it from men of experience, and by attending to it, each for himself, throughout his whole life, studying what food or drink, or what exercise, was most suitable for him, and how he might act in regard to them so as to enjoy the best health; for he said it would be difficult for a person who thus attended to himself to find a physician that would tell better than himself what was conducive to his health.

Xenophon, *The Memorabilia of Socrates*

We Should Try to Free Ourselves from Desire

You, who do not even wait for the natural desire of gratification, but fill yourself with all manner of dainties before you have an appetite for them, eating before you are hungry, drinking before you are thirsty, procuring cooks that you may eat with pleasure, buying costly wines that you may drink with pleasure, and running about seeking for snow in summer, while, in order to sleep with pleasure, you prepare not only soft beds, but couches, and rockers under your couches, for you do not desire sleep in consequence of labor, but in consequence of having nothing to do; you force the sensual inclinations before they require gratification, using every species of contrivance for the purpose, and abusing male and female, for thus it is that you treat your friends, insulting their modesty at night, and making them sleep away the most useful part of their day.

Xenophon, *The Memorabilia of Socrates*

He was not only superior to all corporeal pleasures, but also to those attendant on the acquisition of money.

Xenophon, *The Memorabilia of Socrates*

So frugal was he, that I do not know whether anyone could not earn ... sufficient to have satisfied Socrates.

Xenophon, *The Memorabilia of Socrates*

Do you think that a philosopher will care very much about what are called pleasures, such as the pleasures of eating and drinking? ... Or about the pleasures of sexual passion?

Plato, *Phædo*

The soul of a philosopher will consider that it is the office of philosophy to set her free.... She gains for herself peace from worldly things, and follows reason and ever abides in it, contemplating what is true and divine and real, and fostered by them.

Plato, *Phædo*

But Pleasure Too Should Not Be Despised

Another person saying that he ate without pleasure, "Acumenus," said Socrates, "prescribes an excellent remedy for that disease." The other asking, "What sort of remedy?" "To abstain from eating," said Socrates; "for he says that, after abstaining, you will live with more pleasure, less expense, and better health."

Xenophon, *The Memorabilia of Socrates*

We Should Try to Free Ourselves from Vengeance

We ought not to repay wrong with wrong or do harm to any man, no matter what we may have suffered from him.

Plato, *Crito*

And We Should Not Fear Death

To fear death, my friends, is only to think ourselves wise, without being wise; for it is to think that we know what we do not know. For everything that men can tell, death may be the greatest good that can happen to them; but they fear it as if they knew quite well that it was the greatest of evils. And what is

this but that shameful ignorance of thinking that we know what we do not know?

Plato, *The Apology*

He who is truly a man, ought not to care
about living a certain time; . . . he leaves all
that to God and considers in what way he
can spend his appointed term.

Plato, *Gorgias*

Do you think that a spirit full of lofty thoughts,
and privileged to contemplate all time, and
all existence, can possibly attach any great
importance to this life? "No, it is impossible." Then such a person will not regard
death as a formidable thing, will he?

Plato, *The Republic*

Note regarding the quoted material used in this chapter:

The Apology, Philebus, Euthyphron, an updated version of translation
by F. J. Church.
Gorgias, an updated version of translation by Benjamin Jowett.
The Republic, an updated version of translation by J. L. Davies and
D. J. Vaughan.
Theætetus, an updated version of translation by Benjamin Jowett.
The Memorabilia of Socrates, an updated version of translation by
J. S. Watson.

Chapter 3

Aristotle

(384–322 BCE)

P EOPLE INFLUENCED BY Judaism and its related
religions of Christianity and Islam tend to think
of ethics as the study of right versus wrong. The
ancient Greeks, including Aristotle, defined it instead
as the study of the good versus the bad, a broader
conception that incorporates right versus wrong but
extends well beyond it.

The principal task of Aristotle's ethics is to define
and illustrate the concept of *eudaimonia*. This
ancient Greek word has traditionally been translated
as "happiness," but this is arguably misleading. In the
text that follows, *eudaimonia* is translated as "the

best life," which is probably closer to what Aristotle meant. He was trying to think through the problem of how we should live and, by doing so, define the agathon "good" that we should be aiming for if we want "the best life."

Another key word for Aristotle is *arête*. This is usually translated as virtue. We have reluctantly kept this translation, but need to warn the reader that *arête* does not mean virtue in the same sense that we moderns often use that word. The problem once again arises from our tendency to view the world through the lens of Judaeo, Judaeo-Christian, or Judaeo-Islamic values.

In all these religions, virtue commonly refers to fixed rules of right and wrong. We are virtuous when we follow God's explicit (written) command and fall into vice when we do not. Aristotle's idea of arête is different. It can be translated as virtue, in the sense of a meritorious action, something in which we can take pride. It can also be translated as skill or mastery or an example of the highest practical intelligence.

Aristotle knew that the greatest Homeric heroes were thought by most ancient Greeks to exemplify *arête*, and Homeric heroes were certainly not always virtuous in a Christian or Muslim sense. So, as you read further about virtue and the virtues, please keep in mind that Aristotle is not describing saints, but rather people who are masterful in a worldly way.

Just to make this a little more complicated, there are times when Aristotle does speak of virtue and vice in the familiar voice of a quasi-Judaeo-preacher. For example, he condemns adultery in strong terms. But this is the exception. Usually the emphasis is on sorting out the good from the bad through reason and experience, not on following fixed moral rules.

Like most philosophers, Aristotle was a logician. Indeed, he is usually credited with the invention of formal logic. He relied on logic to arrive at his conclusions, and readers may feel that the logic occasionally gets lost in an overgrown thicket of verbal distinctions. The French philosopher Michel de Montaigne (1533–1592) deprecated this tendency of philosophy in his *Essays*:

> [The deductive method is all] preambles, definitions, classifications . . . etymologies [and] disputes . . . about words. . . . A stone is a body. But if you press the point: and what is a body?—a substance—and what is a substance? and so on. . . . One [merely] substitutes one word for another, that is . . . less well understood. [Such verbal gymnastics are followed by]:

> scattering and chopping . . . small questions [until] the world teem[s] . . . with uncertainties and disputes. . . . Have you ever seen

[someone] trying to divide a mass of quicksilver into a number of parts? The more he presses and squeezes it, and tries to bring it under control, the more [it] keeps breaking and diversifying itself indefinitely. So it is here.... By the subdivision of these subtleties, we [accomplish little]. . . .

Philosophy's object is to calm tempests of the souls, to teach ... virtue, which does not, as the [logicians] allege, stand on the top of a sheer mountain, rugged and inaccessible. Those who have approached it have found it, on the contrary, dwelling on a fair, fertile plateau, from which it can clearly see all things below it. . . . Anyone who knows the way can get there by shady, grassy, and sweetly flowering paths, pleasantly and up an easy and smooth incline. . . .*

Montaigne was an anti-logician, a pure empiricist who wanted to observe and study the world, find the best examples and practices, and learn from that. Aristotle was different; he was no anti-logician. Like all the followers of Socrates, he was excited by the prospect of using logic to reason through life's most perplexing questions. But, like Montaigne, Aristotle was also an empiricist, an observer, a collector of evidence, an

---

* Michel de Montaigne, *Essays*, translated by J. M. Cohen (London: Penguin Books, 1953).

organizer of observed facts, indeed one of the earliest empiricists.* As he said:

> We must consider our conclusion not only
> in terms of our premises, but also in light
> of further evidence. If a conclusion is true,
> all the data harmonize, but with a false one
> the facts soon clash.

Good empiricist that he was, he knew that any answers he developed about the nature of "the best life" would not be precise:

> It is the hallmark of an educated man to
> look for precision in a class of things only
> insofar as the nature of the subject admits.
> In other words, it is equally foolish to de-
> mand scientific proofs from a rhetorician as
> it is to settle for probable reasoning from a
> mathematician. And so we must be content
> to sketch the truth roughly and in outline.

Individuals would also have to use judgment in apply-ing this truth both to themselves and to circumstances:

> That we must act according to the right rule
> is a common principle. . . . But we must agree

---

* Who was the first empiricist in recorded history? Perhaps the Indian prince, Gautama, the Buddha, who was startlingly empiricist in his approach, and lived before Aristotle.

that matters concerned with conduct and questions of what is good for us have no fixity, no more than do matters of health. The agents themselves must in each case consider what is appropriate to the occasion, just as in the arts of medicine and navigation.

Aristotle is not only an empiricist; but he also has abundant common sense. For example, he stresses that it is not enough to identify "the best life." One must actually live it:

At the Olympic Games, it is not the most beautiful or the strongest who are crowned, but those who compete, for it is from these the victors emerge. In the same way, it is necessary to act in order to win—rightly win— the noble and good things in life.

This common sense is not lofty. It is accompanied by a gritty realism:*

We identify the best activities with the best life. But in order to engage in these best activities, we also require some external goods, as it is impossible, or at least not easy, to perform noble acts without the proper equipment. In many actions we rely on friends,

_____

* In the everyday, not the philosophical sense.

riches, and political power as instruments; likewise, lacking certain things (e.g., good birth, good children, beauty) takes the luster from the best life.

The man who is very ugly in appearance, ill born, or solitary and childless is unlikely to live the best life (this would be still less likely if he had thoroughly bad children or friends, or had lost good children or friends by death). The best life depends on a degree of prosperity.

Aristotle is not, however, a simple materialist in his interpretation of good living:

If great events turn out ill, they crush and maim the best life, bringing pain and hindering activities. Yet even in this case, nobility shines through when a man bears with resignation many great misfortunes, not because he is insensible to pain but through nobility and greatness of soul.

If, as we said, activities are what gives life its character, no man who seeks the best life can become completely miserable, for he will never commit acts that are hateful and mean. The man who is truly good and wise always makes the best of circumstances.

This is so even should he suffer misfortunes like Priam's.*

Lack of money or other material blessings can be a problem—nevertheless these are at best means to an end. What then is our end, our real purpose, as human beings seeking to live the best life? As Aristotle says:

Wealth is evidently not the good we are seeking; it is merely useful and desired for the sake of something else. Pleasure, honor, and contemplation are more likely to be ends, since they are loved for themselves. But not even these are ultimate ends. . . .

[An ultimate end] might be discovered if we could first ascertain the function of man. Have the carpenter and the tanner certain functions or activities, while men in general have none? Given that an eye, hand, foot—indeed, each of the body parts—evidently has a particular function, may one not reason that the whole man has a function apart from all these? If so, what can it be?

We suggest that the unique function of man is to act, from the depths of his soul, in accord with a rational principle, which means

---

* The king of ancient Troy whose city was sacked by the Greeks.

in accord with virtue—or if there is more than one virtue, in accord with the best and most complete of these.

Aristotle then proceeds to define what virtue is and what the virtues are:

Let us now examine the specific virtues, exploring what they are; what sort of things they are concerned with. . . .

First, let us observe that right action is neither too little nor too much. For example, both excessive exercise and an utter lack of exercise destroy one's strength; similarly, consuming drink or food above or below a certain amount destroys the health, while that which is proportionate produces, increases, and preserves health. So too, in the case of temperance, courage, and the other virtues. The man who fears and flies from everything, not standing his ground against anything, becomes a coward. The man who fears nothing at all but goes to meet every danger becomes rash. Similarly, the man who indulges in every pleasure and abstains from none becomes self-indulgent, while the man who shuns every pleasure becomes ascetic. Both temperance and courage are preserved by the mean.

Finding this mean requires effort. By abstaining from pleasures we become temperate, and it is when we have become so that we are most able to abstain. Similarly in the case of courage, by being habituated to despise things that are terrible and to stand our ground against them, we become brave. And it is when we have become brave that we shall be most able to stand up to terrible things. . . .

We must also examine the things by which we ourselves are most easily carried away. Some of us tend to one thing, some to another; this is recognizable from the pleasure and pain we feel. We must drag ourselves toward the contrary extreme, for in order to achieve the intermediate state we must pull well away from error, as people do when straightening bent sticks. . . .

None of the moral virtues come to us by nature. If they did, we would have no choice about them. Neither by nature nor contrary to nature do the moral virtues arise in us; rather, we are adapted by nature to develop them, and they are made perfect by habit. . . . It makes no small difference whether we form habits of one kind or another from our very youth; indeed, it makes all the difference. . . .

Virtue is a manifestation of good character, which enables us to live well, just as good eyes enable us to see well. Good character reflects a mean, but not an arithmetic mean. For instance, if ten is many of something and two is few, six is the intermediate. Exceeding and exceeded by an equal amount, it is intermediate according to arithmetical proportion. But the intermediate relative to us is not so calculated. If ten pounds of food are too much for a particular person to eat and two too little, it does not follow that the trainer will order six pounds; for this may be too much for the person who is to take it, or too little—too little for the champion, too much for the beginning athlete.

Not every action or every passion admits of a mean. Some passions have names that already imply vice (e.g., spite, shamelessness, envy); and in the case of actions, adultery, theft, and murder. All of these suggest by their names that they are examples of vice, so that excesses or deficiencies do not apply to them. It is never possible to be right with regard to them; one must always be wrong.

Nor is it better to commit adultery with the right woman, at the right time, and in the right way. Simply to do it is to go wrong. . . .

The concept of the mean cannot be rigidly applied; in some cases the deficiency, in some cases the excess, is more opposed to the mean. For example, it is not rashness, which is an excess, but cowardice, which is a deficiency, that is more opposed to courage. Neither is it asceticism, which is a deficiency, but self-indulgence, which is an excess, that is more opposed to temperance. Since rashness is thought to be more similar to courage, and cowardice more unlike, we oppose the latter to courage; for things that are further from the intermediate are thought to be more contrary to it. In general, we describe as contrary to the mean the direction in which we, as humans, are more likely to go. Therefore self-indulgence, which is an excess, is rightly regarded as more contrary to temperance. . . .

The passions that we possess are in themselves neither virtuous nor the opposite. By passions I mean appetite, anger, fear, confidence, envy, joy, friendly feeling, hatred, longing, emulation, pity—in general, the feelings that accompany pleasure or pain. A man is neither praised nor blamed for feeling anger but rather for *how* he feels anger. Also, we feel anger and fear without choice, but the virtues involve choice. The virtues, therefore, are not passions; nor are they the faculties through which we experience passions: They are, rather, manifestations of character. . . .

Most people, taking refuge in theory, imagine that they are philosophers and will become good "by thinking about it"; in this, they behave like patients who listen attentively to their doctors but follow through on none of the things prescribed for them. As the latter will not be made well in body by such a course of treatment, the former will not be made well in soul by such a course of philosophy.

So there we have it. The purpose of our life is to shape our character to reflect the virtues. If we do so, this will give us "the best life," unless some terrible calamity intervenes, and if it does, character will help us bear calamity with the least pain. This is both a highly idealistic and a highly realistic philosophy of life. It is not surprising that it should have held such a central place in both intellectual and moral history.

Biographical Sketch

Aristotle was born at Stagirus in northern Greece (Thrace). His father served as a physician to the King of Macedon, the grandfather of Alexander the Great, whom Aristotle would later tutor.

Following his father's death, the then 17-year-old Aristotle traveled to Athens where he became a pupil of Plato's. When Plato died in 347 BCE, Aristotle was not chosen to succeed him as head of the Academy, and accepted an invitation to transfer to Atarneus and Assos, where he married Pythias, niece of the King Hermeas. At some later point, Aristotle married again, this time to Herphyllis, who bore him a son, Nicomachus, hence the title *Nicomachean Ethics*, a treatise addressed to his son.

After Hermeas was captured by the Persians, through treachery, and executed, Aristotle moved to Mytilene, and then to Macedon, having accepted the invitation to tutor Alexander, then 13. After five years, the two must have become close, because Alexander sent him specimens to study as Alexander traveled across Asia in his career of conquest. Once Alexander had embarked on his Kingship and military campaign, Aristotle returned to Athens where he set up his own school, the Lyceum. Because of Aristotle's habit of walking as he lectured, his followers were called Peripatetics.

The death of Alexander in 323 BCE brought an anti-Macedonian reaction in Athens. As part of this, Aristotle became endangered, and he chose to depart so that the Athenians would not sin twice against philosophy—a reference to the execution of Socrates. Not long after, in Chalcis, on the nearby island of Euboea, he died from a stomach complaint.

All of Aristotle's published work perished. Some of his unpublished work, including the *Nicomachean Ethics*, survived. This large trove of material, so original and groundbreaking, is nevertheless somewhat disorganized and repetitive. One idea is that it constitutes his lecture notes. Another idea is that it is notes jotted down by students as Aristotle taught. Even this material almost disappeared forever. It was preserved by Islamic scholars and republished in the 9th century. Eventually, it was rediscovered in Europe and became immensely influential. Aristotle was equally a philosopher (including an economist) and early scientist, and remains one of the greatest minds of world history.

Note regarding the quoted material used in this chapter:

Nicomachean Ethics, an updated version of translation by W. D. Ross.

Chapter 4

Epicurus

(342–270 BCE)

E PICUREANISM AND STOICISM occupy a unique place in the history of human thought. They were philosophies, not religions, but they came to take the place of religion with the more educated ancient Greeks and Romans.

The ancients tended to emphasize what was different among the two. They were sometimes regarded as mortal enemies locked in conflict as they sought allegiance from at least the educated public. Partisans of one or the other would claim their beliefs were being completely distorted, as they often were. For example, Epicureanism was charged with espousing a gross hedonism, when it actually espoused the opposite.

14. We live most happily if we live quietly apart from the multitude of other people, provided that we have adequate protection from them and also enough to meet our basic material needs.

15. It is not difficult to have enough to live, but we can never have enough to suit our vain fancies.

17. By living justly, we can enjoy peace of mind; by living unjustly we will never achieve it.

18. It is pleasures themselves—along with everything that accompanies them—that destroys our peace of mind.

20. Our pleasure seeking has no limit. We always want more and for an unlimited time. Only the mind, understanding the reality of our life and escaping terrors of all kinds, can give us a complete and perfect life within the time that we are given. Even at the hour of death, when circumstances require us to depart, the mind can help us enjoy whatever of life remains to us.

21. The mind can help us grasp how easy it is to lift our life out of want and make our life complete and perfect. . . .

27. Wisdom teaches us that nothing is more important for our happiness than making and keeping friends.

35. Before breaking laws or behaving unjustly to others, consider that you will never know when you might

pay a price. Even if you have escaped detection or retribution ten thousand times, even at the very end of your life, you could yet be unmasked.

36. The rules of justice apply to everyone and are required for us to cooperate and live together. But circumstances, conditions, and locales differ, which will affect their application.

Letter to Pythocles

When we say that pleasure is the objective, we do not mean the pleasures of the profligate or the pleasures of sensuality, as we are understood to do by some through ignorance, prejudice, or willful misinterpretation. By "pleasure" we mean the absence of pain in the body and of turmoil in the mind. The pleasurable life is not continuous drinking, dancing, and sex; nor the enjoyment of fish or other delicacies of an extravagant table. It is sober reasoning which searches out the motives for all choice and avoidance, and rejects those beliefs which lay open the mind to the greatest disturbance:

> The beginning of wisdom and the greatest good is taking care to avoid undesirable consequences. Prudence in life is more precious than philosophy itself, for all the other virtues spring from it. It is impossible to live pleasurably without also living prudently,

> honestly, and justly; [nor is it possible to
> lead a life of prudence, honor and justice]
> and not live pleasantly. We cannot expect a
> pleasant life without practicing the virtues;
> the two are inseparable.

Note that this is one of the earliest and most beautiful
expressions of the doctrine of living sustainably and iden-
tifies sustainability with morality as well as happiness.

Vatican Sayings

XVII.   It might seem that a young person should be
        happiest, but it is actually an older person who
        has lived a good life. A young person is full of
        life and strength but is unstable, easily swept
        this or that way by fortune. An old man who
        has led a good life has found an anchorage, like
        a ship in the port.

XXIV.   Dreams are not from God nor do they prophesy
        anything. They are just images conjured up by
        the brain.

XXV.   Living in what is called poverty may give us
        great wealth; unlimited wealth just brings us
        what is really poverty.

XLI.   We should try to laugh and philosophize even
        while we go about our everyday life and fulfilling

our duties. We cannot remind ourselves of the true philosophy too often.

XLIV. The wise person who understands life prefers to give than to receive. Self-sufficiency is a treasure.

LI. Yes, your body drives you to the pleasures of love. So long as you do not break laws or good customs or harm others or harm your own body or waste what little money you have, go ahead. But in reality you will face one of these constraints. Do not expect rewards from these pleasures; you will be lucky if you escape unharmed.

LV. The only way to overcome mistakes is to be grateful for what has gone well and to realize that the past can never be undone.

LVIII. Public life and politics are actually a prison for us.

LXIII. Frugality can also be overdone. A person who disregards this is no different from someone who falls into excess.

LXX. It is best to avoid doing anything which we would not want revealed to others.

Fragments in Greek Literature

54. The chief purpose of philosophy is to help us avoid unnecessary suffering. Just as medicine is supposed to help heal the body, philosophy should help heal our mind.

83. A wise person who has understood life will be just as good alone as in company.

Biographical Sketch

Born on the island of Samos in the end of 342 or the beginning of 341 BCE, not long after the death of Plato, Epicurus traveled to Athens at age 18 for more schooling, but soon returned home. In 307, he returned to Athens to establish his school, which was referred to as "The Garden," because it was located in one, and remained there for the rest of his life.

He and his followers lived very simply, the opposite of the hedonism with which they were charged. Plain water, a little wine, bread, a little cheese, and a few olives were the general fare. Each person owned his own property. They sought to avoid political life, which was unexpected and controversial in a Greek city-state, on the grounds that it featured unnecessary worries and personal risks without accomplishing much good. On the other hand, kindness and charity were extolled.

Epicurus died from what may have been kidney stones or some other urinary or digestive disorder in 270 BCE. Throughout that ordeal, he is reported to have maintained his usual peace of mind and even temper. He reasoned that death should not be feared, precisely because we would feel nothing once dead and there could be no further suffering once the flame of life was gone. In other words, the likely absence of an afterlife was a blessing.

Note regarding the quoted material used in this chapter:

The Principal Doctrines, Letter to Pythocles, Fragments in Greek Literature, Vatican Sayings, translation by Hunter Lewis, 2017.

Chapter 5

Epictetus
(55–135 CE)

T**HE LIFE OF** Epictetus is quite obscure. He was a slave for the early part of his life, owned by a freedman of the Emperor Nero, reputed to have come from Asia Minor (now Turkey) and reputed to have been lame. His owner Epaphroditus apparently thought it would be an adornment to his household to have a philosopher resident there, so sent Epictetus to be trained by the Stoic teacher C. Musonius Rufus. At some point, perhaps after his owner was executed by the Emperor Domitian, he became free and began to teach himself, but in Nicopolis in Greece. He lived to an old age, remained unmarried, but is said to have adopted an orphan child. His pupil Arrian apparently took the notes which were later assembled as *The Discourses* and *The Handbook*. The two together are the central documents of ancient Stoicism. Nothing by the founder of Stoicism, Zeno, remains. *The Memoirs* of the Stoic Emperor Marcus Aurelius and *The Consolations of Philosophy* by Boethius, written much later, are equally or more famous, but are less central to understanding the teachings.

The Discourses

Book 15.11–13

You . . . must toil, you must get the better of . . . your desires. . . . When you have done all these things, you will have . . . serenity, freedom and an undisturbed mind. Do not, like children, try to be at one time a philosopher, a tax-collector, a rhetorician, one of Caesar's procurators. These are not compatible. You must be one person, either good or bad. You must be either a philosopher or a layman.

The Handbook

1. Some things are in our power, others are not. In our power are opinion, desire (moving toward a thing), aversion (turning from a thing); and in a word, whatever are our own actions. Not in our power are the body, property, reputation, offices

(magisterial power), and in a word, whatever are not caused entirely by our own actions.

The things in our power are by nature free, not subject to restraint nor hindrance. Things not in our power make slaves of us, subject us to restraint, put us in the power of others. If you mistakenly think the things which make us slaves to be free, the things which are in the power of others to be your own, you will be hindered, you will lament, you will be disturbed, you will blame both gods and men. But if you recognize that which is your own to be your own, and if you recognize that which is another's, as it really is, to belong to another, no one will ever compel you, no one will hinder you, you will never blame anyone else, you will accuse no one else, you will do nothing involuntarily (against your will), no one will harm you, you will have no enemy, and you will suffer no real harm.

If you wish to aim at such great things, remember that you must not be content with a small effort. You must leave some things alone entirely, and postpone others for the present. If you wish for power and wealth also, perhaps you will gain neither the one nor the other. You will certainly fail in those things through which alone happiness and freedom are secured.

Do not delay. Begin to practice saying to every harsh appearance: You are merely an appearance, and in no manner what you appear to be. Then examine it by the rules which you possess, and by this first and chiefly, whether it relates to the things which are in our power or to the things which are not in our power: and if it relates to anything which is not in our power, be ready to tell yourself that it does not concern you.

2. Remember that anyone who fails in a desire is unfortunate and unhappy, and so is anyone who fails to avoid something that one wishes to avoid. If you attempt to avoid disease or death or poverty, you will be unhappy. It is best to avoid what is in your power, desire, completely for the present. . . .

5. Men are disturbed not by the things which happen, but by their opinions concerning those things. For example, death is not so terrible; if it were, it would have seemed so to Socrates. It is the opinion about death, that it is terrible, that makes it terrible.

When then, we are impeded or disturbed or grieved, we should not blame others, but ourselves, that is, our opinions. It is the act of an ill-instructed man to blame others for his own bad condition; it is better but still wrong to blame oneself; a wise person blames no one.

8. Do not ask that events should happen as you wish, but rather wish that events should happen as they do, and you will have a tranquil flow of life.

15. In life you ought to behave as at a banquet. Suppose that something is carried round and is opposite to you. Stretch out your hand and take a portion with decency. Suppose that it passes by you. Do not detain it. Suppose that it is not yet come to you. In that case, do not desire it, but wait till it is opposite to you. Do so with respect to children, with respect to a spouse, with respect to public offices, with respect to wealth, and you will be a worthy partner of the banquets of the gods. But if you take none of the things that are set before you, and even despise them, then you will be not only a fellow banqueter with the gods, but also a partner with them in power. For by acting thus Diogenes and Heraclitus and those like them were deservedly divine, and were so called.

28. You would not wish to put your body in the power of any man whom you fell in with on the way. So why would you put your mind in the power of any man whom you meet, with the result that if he should revile you, you would be disturbed and troubled. Are you not ashamed by this?

30. Does a brother wrong you? If so, maintain your own position toward him, and do not examine what he

is doing, but instead what you must do to make your own will in conformity with nature. Another person will not damage you, unless you choose to be damaged, and you will only be damaged when you think you have been damaged.

33. Prescribe some character and some form to yourself, which you shall observe both when you are alone and when you meet with others.

And let silence be the general rule, or only say what is necessary to say, and in few words. And avoid the common subjects, gladiators, horse-races, athletes, eating or drinking. Especially avoid discussing other people, blaming them, praising them, comparing them.

And keep your laughter confined, do not display it on many occasions, nor in excess.

Refuse altogether to take an oath, if it is possible. If it is not, refuse as far as you are able.

Avoid banquets given by strangers and by ignorant persons. But if ever there is occasion to join in them, let your attention be carefully fixed, that you do not slip into the manners of the vulgar. Accept those gifts which help us maintain the body, such as food, drink, clothing, housing, and slaves, but exclude anything which is for show or luxury.

As to pleasure with women, abstain as far as you can before marriage. If you indulge in it, do it in the way which is conformable to custom. Do not, however, be disagreeable to those who indulge in these pleasures or reprove them; and do not boast that you do not indulge in them yourself.

If someone has reported to you that someone else speaks ill of you, do not try to defend yourself. Rather reply: I have other faults not mentioned.

It is not necessary to go to the theaters often. If there is a proper occasion to go, do not show yourself to be a partisan of anyone. Abstain entirely from shouts and laughter at anything or person, or a display of violent emotions. Whatever you attend, try to remain grave and sedate, but also avoid making yourself critical or disagreeable.

When you are going to visit any of those who are in great power, tell yourself that you will not find the man at home, that you will be excluded, that the door will not be opened to you, that the man will not care about you. And if with all this it is your duty to visit him, bear what happens, and never say to yourself that it was not worth the trouble. For this is silly, and marks the character of a man who is offended by mere external events.

In company try to avoid speaking of your own actions or dangers. It feels natural for you to make mention of yourself, but it is not so pleasant to others to hear what has happened to you. Take care also not to try to provoke laughter; this is a slippery slope toward vulgar habits, and will also reduce the respect of your neighbors. It is also a poor idea to engage in obscene talk.

41. It is a mark of a meanness to dwell on things which concern the body, such as exercise, eating, drinking, elimination, and copulation. These things are subordinate; let all your care be directed to the mind.

42. When any person treats you ill or speaks ill of you, do not overreact. It is not possible for others to do what seems right to you, only what seems right to them. If they are wrong, they will be hurt. Be mild then to those who revile you. Remind yourself that it seemed so to them.

44. These ideas are not factual or logical: I am richer than you, therefore I am better than you; I am more eloquent than you, therefore I am better than you. On the contrary, these are factual: I am richer than you, therefore my possessions are greater than yours; I am more eloquent than you, therefore my speech is superior to yours. But you are neither possession nor speech.

48. Uninstructed people never expect profit or harm, but from outside themselves. Philosophers

understand that all advantage and all harm arises from within ourselves. Philosophers should not care what others think, but should guard against their own minds as they would an enemy lying in ambush.

Fragments

20. Those whose bodies are in good condition are able to withstand heat and cold; and so, likewise, those whose souls are in the right condition can bear anger, and grief, and immoderate joy, and all other emotions.

34. If one should overstep the mean, the most enjoyable things would become the least so.

35. No man is free who is not master of himself.

Note regarding the quoted material used in this chapter:

The Discourses; Fragments, an updated version of translation by Robin Hard.
The Handbook, an updated version of translation by George Long.

Part Three

Modern Moral Thinkers

Chapter 6

Desiderius Erasmus

(1466–1536)

DESIDERIUS ERASMUS WAS the second son of a "celibate" Catholic priest and a woman named Margaret living in Gouda, Holland. While still a teenager, both parents died of bubonic plague, and he had to seek shelter in a monastery, where eventually in 1492 he became a priest himself.

From these lowly beginnings, Erasmus rose to become one of the most famous and influential figures in Europe. He is considered by many to be the preeminent intellectual figure of the Renaissance. Moreover, as we shall explore below, there are elements of teachings that are timeless and perhaps especially relevant to the 21st century.

As soon as he could, Erasmus abandoned monastery life and set off as an itinerant scholar, living very frugally and relying on a succession of often undependable rich and powerful patrons to pay his way. As his fame increased, patrons eventually included a pope and many princes, including Henry VIII of England, but other popes and princes condemned him, including the powerful Charles V, Emperor of Spain, the Netherlands, Austria-Hungary, and much else, who forbade reading his *Colloquies* on penalty of death.

The *Colloquies* was only one of Erasmus's mountain of books, pamphlets, and letters. The writer and scholar was also a journalist, propagandist, and promoter who caught the first wave of book printing, and fed it with work upon work, many produced at top speed mainly off the top of his head.

The books and tracts fed to the voracious new printing presses were often, by the standards of the day, popular works, despite being written in Latin. Some others, such as a new edition of the New Testament, required years of painstaking and careful scholarship. Creating a new translation of holy scripture, based on the original Greek text, was a very bold venture that could easily have led to his excommunication from the Church or execution. Many others of the same era died for undertaking translations not authorized by the Church; the Church did not generally favor new translations, particularly into common languages.

By the time of his death at approximately age 69, plagued by kidney stones, gout, and other painful ills acquired over a lifetime of faltering health, finally felled by dysentery, no priest by his side or last rites administered, an estimated three-quarters of a million copies of his books had been printed. This would have made him a bestseller even in modern times, but given that most of the population of Europe at the time was illiterate both in Latin and in their own tongue, it is almost unimaginable, and shows what a sea change printing brought to the world.

It is surprising that Erasmus succeeded in living as long as he did, given the powerful enemies he made, including toward the end of his life the menacing clerics surrounding the Spanish throne who later became infamous as the Spanish Inquisition. After Luther's break with Rome in 1517, his life was always at risk, as the world slid into the religious wars and massacres that he so strongly opposed.

Erasmus's personal convictions, such as his opposition to tyranny, intolerance, and war, especially religious tyranny, intolerance, and war, are often laid out in the boldest headlines. But sometimes his position is a bit harder to discern. He has often been called a humanist, or a Christian humanist, but these terms obscure as much as they reveal.

Was Erasmus a doctrinally orthodox Christian? He had to be cautious for his own safety, but, as we shall see, took considerable risks. He generally described himself as a Church reformer, intent on rooting out hypocrisy and corruption and putting faith and works ahead of ceremony and ritual. He suggested that married sexual relations might be superior to celibacy. He proposed an end to burning books and people and otherwise punishing people for their beliefs or for alleged witchcraft. But he always insisted throughout that doctrinally he was a conventional believer.

In 1513, after Pope Julius II died, Erasmus dared to write in his satire *Julius Exclusus* that "fraud, usury, and cunning made you Pope" and to excoriate both his military campaigns and the harsh taxes imposed on peasants to pay for them. The next pope, Leo X, a Medici from Florence, was relatively tolerant and very friendly to Erasmus, but increased the sale of indulgences to raise more money for Rome and by doing so helped to provoke Luther's rebellion.

Erasmus's most famous book, *The Praise of Folly*, published in 1511, ruthlessly satirized popes, priests, and all the foibles and failures of the Church in the years immediately preceding the Protestant Reformation, followed by the Church's Counter-Reformation. It included this passage:

> All Christian religion seems to have a kind
> of alliance with Folly and to have no accord
> with wisdom. The first founders of it were

plain, simple persons and most bitter enemies of learning. . . . There are no fools more
out of the way than those whom the zeal of
Christian religion has once swallowed up;
so that they waste their estates, neglect inju-
ries, suffer themselves to be cheated, see no
difference between friends and enemies, ab-
hor pleasure, suffer poverty, vigils, tears, labors, reproaches, loathe life, and wish death
above all things; in short, they seem sense-
less to common understanding, as if their
minds lived elsewhere and not in their own
bodies; and what else is this if not mad?

You must not think it so strange if the apostles seemed to be drunk with new wine, or
if Paul appeared to Festus to be mad. . . .
When they come to themselves, they tell
you they know not where they have been,
whether in the body or out of the body, or
sleeping; nor do they remember what they
have heard, seen, spoken, or done, and only
know this, as it were in a mist or dream, that
they were the most happy while they were
so out of their wits. And therefore they are
sorry they are come to themselves again and
desire nothing more than this kind of mad-
ness, to be perpetually mad.

Is this damning or actually praising Christianity? We must also keep in mind that this is not supposed to be Erasmus speaking. This is the alleged author of the book, the goddess Folly. Moreover, there was a tradition dating from at least medieval times that court jesters, human embodiments of Folly, were allowed to say just about anything, without threat of punishment by either Church or prince, so long as the message is meant to be humorous.

At other times, Erasmus staunchly defended Christianity, orthodox Catholic belief, and especially the authority of the Catholic Church independent of scripture. And although he initially welcomed Luther as a reformer, he quickly warned that the religious reform movement should stay inside the Church, or would soon be twisted and exploited by secular rulers for their own purposes. When in 1525, 100,000 German peasants rebelled against their local overlords, thinking that Luther would support them, but were instead tortured, hanged, and impaled with Luther's blessing, and when Luther endorsed slavery, Erasmus was not surprised by any of it, but was no less appalled. In correspondence and books, he warned Luther that he was bringing on a conflagration that would engulf Europe, as it did, with a third of the German population eventually dying in so-called religious wars and with similar massacres and convulsions taking place elsewhere.

The Praise of Folly was written in only a week and presented as a gift to Erasmus's friend Thomas More. The title in Latin, *Moriae Encomium*, is a clever pun on More's name. More was later executed by King Henry VIII for refusing to support England's break with Rome and was later sainted by the Catholic Church. More's own book *Utopia* (1515) ironically seems to endorse the complete subjection of everyone, in thought and action, to monarch and state, but that, too, may have been intended as satire.

Erasmus's satire did not limit itself to lampooning Christianity and the Church of the day. Speaking in the voice of Folly, and therefore given what the author called "the license to speak the truth without offense," he said:

> A man who has gained understanding pities and laments the insanity of those who are confined to illusions, but they in turn laugh at him as quite mad and throw him out.

> The less skillful anything is, the more admirers it attracts.

> The people are an enormous and powerful monster swayed by absurdities.

> Flattery is the honey and spice of all human intercourse.

> [The] . . . belief in communism of property goes to such lengths that [people] . . .

> pick up anything unguarded and make off with it without a flutter of conscience as if it were theirs by right of law.

> Wisdom makes men weak and apprehensive, and that is why you generally see wise men living in poverty and hunger, whereas fools are rolling in money.

> Since the wise man scorns money, it usually does its best to stay out of his way.

> That academics never know anything for certain at all is clear enough from this fact alone: on every single point they disagree violently and irreconcilably among themselves.

> The most foolish and meanest profession of all is that of merchants, since they seek the meanest goal by the meanest methods: money.

> If rulers had an ounce of good sense, what could be more wretched and repellent to them than the life they lead?

Folly does not just mock or criticize. On occasion, notwithstanding her claim to promote foolishness, Erasmus cannot stop himself from offering some philosophical wisdom:

> Nothing could be further from the truth than the notion that man's happiness resides

in things as they actually are; it depends on opinions. [This is, of course, an echo of Epicurus and Epictetus.]

The chief point of happiness is to wish to be what you actually are.

Can someone who hates himself love anyone else?

Nothing is really enjoyable without someone to share it with.

We should not expect Erasmus to be a modern man. But he was often the first to develop themes that would define modernity. Although skeptical of the masses, he nevertheless sided with them against their rulers. He did not believe in Plato's idea of guardians, ideal rulers who would put the needs of the people first. In *Dulce bellum inexpertis,* he wrote that a ruler is "carnivorous, rapacious, a brigand, a destroyer, solitary, hated by all, a pest to all . . ." and introduced the idea of limited government as the only possible palliative.

In *Adages Collectanae*, he wrote:

Do we not see that noble cities are erected by the people and destroyed by princes? That a state grows rich by the industry of its citizens and is plundered by the rapacity of its rulers? That good laws are enacted by

representatives of the people and violated
by kings? That the commons love peace and
the monarchs foment war?

In addition, he opposed colonization of other lands by
European powers, a very novel idea at the time.

Perhaps Erasmus's most powerful idea was that of
toleration, of allowing people to think and speak as
they like, because the alternative just leads to needless conflict and violence. Throughout history, rulers have sought to quell dissent on the grounds that
it leads to instability and violence. Erasmus's great
insight, later embodied in the constitution of the
United States, was that individual liberties, perhaps
principal among them free speech, are not only justified on moral grounds. They are also socially stabilizing, because they act as a safety valve. Allowing
people to be free to pursue their own goals without
government interference and practicing toleration
of other people's beliefs and way of life are the basic
requirements of a successful as well as a moral society.

Erasmus hoped for a future world in which people interacted entirely by cooperating, not by prey-
ing on one another, a dream that finally began to be
realized to some degree only in later centuries, in the
form of a world economy. A corollary of this is that
we must overcome the tribal boundaries that our
primitive brains erect and once and for all put an

end to the notion of warfare as a solution to conflict, an idea (and ideal) that he presented with his usual pith and sense:

Erasmus Contra War

What is more foolish than undertaking a struggle from which both sides will emerge more harmed than helped? (*The Praise of Folly*)

War is inhuman, insane, noxious, unjust, and impious. (Ibid.)

... Is it possible for a man to draw a murderous sword and plunge it into his brother's vitals without loss of the supreme charity which in accordance with Christ's teaching every Christian owes his neighbor. (Ibid.)

Since the Christian Church was founded on blood, strengthened by blood and increased in blood, they continue to manage its affairs by the sword as if Christ has perished and can no longer protect his own people in his own way. War is something so monstrous that it befits wild beasts rather than men, so crazy that the poets even imagine that it is let loose by Furies, so deadly that it sweeps like a plague through the world, so unjust that it is generally best carried on by the worst type of bandit, so impious that it is quite alien to Christ; and yet they leave everything to devote themselves to war. . . . (Ibid.)

War is a treat for those who have not tried it. (*Adages*)

What is it that drives the whole human race, not merely Christians, to such a pitch of frenzy that they will undergo such effort, expense, and danger for the sake of mutual destruction? . . . Even when the war is over, this moral corruption is bound to linger for many years. (Letter to Antoon van Bergen)

Who will not agree that there is nothing more cruel in the world than the slaying of one man by another? But it is also in the evil nature of war that it carries off none more frequently than the very best and most deserving of life. . . . ("On The Christian Widow")

War [is a] . . . a kind of encircling ocean of all the evils in the world. ("A Complaint of Peace")

Are you longing for war? First take a look at what peace and war really are. . . . If it is something for admiration when a kingdom is prosperous throughout, with its cities soundly established, lands well cultivated, excellent laws, the best teaching, and the highest moral standards, consider who you will necessarily destroy all this happiness if you go to war.... (Ibid.)

The majority of the common people loathe war and pray for peace; only a handful of individuals, whose evil joys depend on general misery, desire war. (Ibid.)

... The vices of war long precede the actual war and also carry on for a long time afterwards, so that the aftermath of war is almost more loathsome that the war itself, and quite often even the victors regret having fought it. ("Panegyric")

War is now such an accepted thing that people are astonished to find anyone who does not like it, and such a respectable thing that it is wicked and, I might almost say, "heretical" to disapprove of this, which of all things is the most abominable and the most wretched. (*Adages*)

There are some whose only reason for inciting war is to use it as a means to exercise their tyranny over their subjects more easily. (Ibid.)

In 1516, Erasmus read Niccolò Machiavelli's *The Prince*, which justified state aggression and war as an instrument of policy, and responded with his own book, *The Education of a Christian Prince*, which included the following:

> The good and wise prince will try to be at peace with all nations but particularly with his neighbours, who can do much harm if they are hostile and much good if they are friendly; no state can survive for long without good relations with them. . . .
>
> Although the prince will never make any decision hastily, he will never be more hesitant or more circumspect than in starting a war; . . . war breeds war, from a small war a greater is born. . . .[11]

These passages of Erasmus's against aggression and particularly against military aggression have been quoted at length because, along with his plea for individual liberty, free thought and speech, tolerance, and global cooperation, they represent powerful ideals that had not previously even been recognized as ideals, and that continue to be under constant and ferocious assault in today's world.

Note regarding the quoted material used in this chapter:
The Praise of Folly by Desiderius Erasmus, an updated version of translation by John Wilson.

Chapter 7

Michel de Montaigne

(1533–1592)*

I N ORDINARY LANGUAGE, the word *experience* can refer to almost anything. We can and do speak of experiencing logic, emotion, intuition, and so on, as in: "I experienced [the emotion of] falling in love for the first time." But when we speak of sense experience, we are referring to something narrower and more specific: the knowledge that we get directly by seeing, hearing, smelling, tasting, or touching.

Obviously, all of us obtain general knowledge, as well as the knowledge needed to form values, through this

---

* This chapter represents an updated version of material that was first published in Hunter Lewis, *A Question of Values* (San Francisco: Harper Collins, 1990).

avenue of direct sense experience. Some people, however, seem to place considerably greater emphasis on
the testimony of their senses than on other modes of
learning, believing, knowing, and judging. They do not
want to accept the teachings of the Bible or the church
on faith. They do not want to sit in a dark room working through abstruse logical problems. They want to see
and hear it themselves, either on the spot in their own
communities or traveling in foreign lands, or vicariously
through books and films. If a friend or a stranger or the
author of a book tells them something is true, they do
not ask themselves: What authority or logic backs up
this statement? They ask instead whether the alleged
truth corresponds to their own entirely personal sense
experience in this world—and, if it does not, the alleged
truth is quietly but decisively put aside.

High Sense Experience

Montaigne expresses this viewpoint completely.
We cannot pursue his personal beliefs too directly.
We will not find them listed conveniently in some
tract, or laboriously argued in a philosophical tome.
We must be patient and approach his personal beliefs
obliquely by first getting to know the man. For example, when we meet Montaigne in his delightful but
purposefully wandering *Essays* (Montaigne invented
the term *essay*, which originally referred to an attempt

to gain knowledge, especially self-knowledge and moral knowledge), he is wearing silk hose and padded doublet, covered by a wrap of vulture's skin to protect himself against a piercing cold wind as he paces his library on the top floor of a tower, which is itself attached to a fortified manor house perched high on a hill overlooking the rolling, checker-boarded fields of rural Gascony. As he observes,

> I can see below my garden, my courtyard, and much of my house. There I turn the pages now of one book, now of another, without method or plan, reading bits and pieces. Sometimes I think, and sometimes I dictate my thoughts, walking back and forth, as at present.[12]

> On the first [floor of the tower] is my chapel, on the second a bedroom with antechambers, where I often lie down.... My [top floor] library is round, with a bit of flat wall occupied by my table and chair. Being round I can see all my books at once. From this room I can see three ways, and walk sixteen steps.... If I were not averse to trouble (which I try to avoid), I could easily create a place to walk outside on the wall a hundred steps long and twelve wide. Every place of retirement should have somewhere to walk....[13]

> In the past, [the tower] was the most useless
> part of the house. Now I spend most days
> there, and most of the hours of the day. . . .
> It is my kingdom, and I try to rule here ab-
> solutely. . . . Miserable, I think, is a man with
> no place to be alone, where he can conduct
> himself in complete privacy. Rightly ambi-
> tion plagues her votaries by keeping them
> always on display. . . . They do not even have
> privacy in the privy. . . . I think it is much
> more bearable always to be alone than never
> to be able to be so.[14]

A servant breaks the spell of solitude by announc-
ing that an armed horseman is at the gate. Montaigne
recollects that

> I knew his name, and thought he could be
> trusted as a neighbor and distant kinsman.
> I let him in as I do everyone. He stood be-
> fore me, seemingly frightened, with his horse
> hard ridden. His story was that he had been
> ambushed by an enemy, someone I also rec-
> ognized and knew to be feuding with him.
> He said that, caught unawares and outnum-
> bered, he had fled to my keep. He was wor-
> ried about his men, whom he thought lost.
> I innocently did my best to comfort, assure,
> and refresh him.

Shortly came four or five of his soldiers similarly frightened and out of breath, asking to be let in. Then more, and still more, coming to 25 or 30, all pretending to have escaped an enemy. I began to be suspicious; I was not ignorant of the age I lived in, how much my house might be envied. But not thinking it wise to have some inside and some outside, I took the simplest course and admitted them all.

These men stood in my courtyard, while their leader was with me inside. He saw that he was master of the moment, and could carry out his plan. [Yet] he mounted his horse; and his followers, whose eyes were set on him, to watch for his signal, were amazed to see him ride off and abandon his plan.[15]

In the midst of religious warfare and banditry, plague periodically grips the countryside:

Apprehension . . . is especially part of this disease. You . . . spend your days worrying . . . with your imagination worked to a pitch. [Among the peasants], they all renounced any desire for life. The grapes, which are the main source of wealth in the area, remained on the vines; and each unconcernedly prepared for a death which they expected that night or the next day. . . .

Because they are all dying together at the same time, the young and old, they cease to be astonished, they even cease to lament. I saw some who were afraid of staying behind, as in a dreadful solitude, and I found them only unconcerned about their burial. It appalled them to see bodies about the fields, eaten by the wild animals. Some, while still healthy, were digging their grave; others lay down in theirs while alive; and one of my laborers, even as he was dying, pulled the earth down upon himself with his hands and feet.[16]

Montaigne is spared from plague, but suffers excruciating kidney stones, an inherited affliction which had killed his father:

People... see you sweat with pain, turn pale, tremble... suffer strange contractions and convulsions, the tears dropping from your eyes. You release thick, dark, and dreadful urine, or have it stopped by a sharp rough-edged stone that cruelly pricks and tears bladder or penis; and all the time you are conversing with those around you, your face in an ordinary expression, making light of your suffering, excusing yourself, trying to talk normally.[17]

Notwithstanding these obstacles, and despite long absences from the tower, first to visit Rome by way of Switzerland (where Montaigne views, and rejects, the novelty of using knives and forks instead of fingers at supper) and then to serve as mayor of Bordeaux, the *Essays* are eventually completed. The first two unrevised volumes are presented to Henry III, monarch of France, equally famous for his transvestism, his court *mignons*, his exquisite manners, and his love of learning. A three-volume edition is later presented to the dashing and energetic Henry of Navarre (Henry IV), whom the nobleman has helped ascend the throne. Even the papal censor joins in the praise, although his successors will eventually reconsider and place the work on the Index of Forbidden Books.

Essays: General Approach

In setting down his *Essays*, Montaigne reveals himself as the kind of man who does not stick to the subject, and who does so brilliantly. As the French philosopher Diderot later described his method: "He cares little where he starts from, how he goes, or where he ends up."[18] Topic is piled on topic (idleness, books, smells, even cannibals)—"I take the first subject that comes to me, all are . . . equally good";[19] digression is piled on digression (a discussion of Christian mysticism merges with a crude scatological story, both adorned by abstruse Latin references). The only thread that runs through all these disconnected impressions is the author himself, his mind and life, the former occasionally contradictory, the latter presented without a trace of chronology.

Even in the midst of this melee, however, the reader is not confused or lost. On the contrary, we are carried along by a transparently clear prose; by an easy, relaxed, entertainingly conversational tone; by an absence of artifice or pretension ("I had rather know what [Brutus][20] did in his home than what he did before the Senate"); and above all by a rivetingly honest stream of self-revelation. It is not just that we learn the nobleman's sleeping habits (late to bed and late to rise: "I like to lie on a hard bed alone . . . without my wife"),[21] or bowel habits (early in the morning), or weakness for physical beauty (the chief criterion by which he chooses household servants as well as lady loves), or fondness for animals ("I cannot refuse my dog when he . . . asks me to play with him at an inconvenient time.").[22] It is rather that through this one human being, who has chosen to "spy on himself from close up" with complete objectivity, we are able to learn about ourselves.

A man who is now a doctor tells the story of being unable to consummate his first love affair during high school. In a state of near-tearful collapse, he secretly visits a psychiatrist who tries to be reassuring: Impotence in young men is often curable, though the treatment may take years. Talking sessions ensue, but self-doubt and panic are only further magnified. Then the youth chances on a passage from the *Essays*:

> I consider this problem, which society loves to talk about, to be likely caused by apprehension. I know a man who cannot possibly be considered impotent. He had heard a friend tell of losing his manhood at just the wrong moment. Later when he was at such a moment, the story filled his mind and the same fate befell him. Afterward the memory of it preyed on his mind so that he suffered repeatedly. But he found a remedy. By confessing the problem in advance, he reduced the fear and apprehension, so it did not weigh so much on his mind. By taking this precaution, he found that he was completely cured.[23]

After reading this passage, the young man is instantly cured.

Attack on Christianity and Logic

The author would assure us that there is no message at all buried among the charming intimacies and digressions of the *Essays*, that he has reached no "conclusions,"[24] that he is not "well enough instructed to instruct anyone else,"[25] that his work is "frivolous"[26] and of "little weight." But such aristocratic subterfuges must be set aside. The *Essays* are not at all what they appear. They are at once a repudiation both of faith in a higher authority and of logic, the two reigning paradigms of the time, and the most complete exposition yet offered of an alternative, an approach to forming values based primarily on personal sense experience.

Montaigne does not directly attack the idea of faith in a higher authority, much less the all-powerful spiritual authority of his day, the Catholic church of France. To do so would bring himself and his family to ruin. As he tells a favorite lady: "I speak the truth, not so much as I would prefer, but as much as I dare; and as I become older, I become a little more daring."[27] Besides, in his view the right way to deal with imperious spiritual authorities, Catholicism included, is not to contest them; opposition just makes them wax hotter and stronger. The best approach is to ignore them, to show them a tolerant, even an affectionate, respect, and then to do as you please.

Nor does the nobleman want to interfere with anyone else's beliefs. If you think you need God or the church, or an infallible book, that is all right. Indeed, popular religion is conceded to have two indisputable advantages, at least in the short run: Not only does it provide answers to questions that are otherwise unanswerable, but it also helps you discipline yourself and control passions that might otherwise prove uncontrollable. In the long run, however, too many answers, in a world where answers are not really available, may become a sort of drug. Like other drugs, it may lead to a cycle of craven dependence alternating with boundless pride, a deadly combination that virtually guarantees misery for believer and unbeliever alike. What people really need, according to Montaigne, is just the reverse: an independent spirit tempered by humility and modesty. Such a spirit may choose to worship a God, but not a God who "fears . . . is angry . . . loves"[28] or otherwise suffers "agitations and emotions" common to us. Better still is to make no assumptions, to remain "doubtful and undecided,"[29] to rest one's head on the "soft and easy and wholesome . . . pillow [of] ignorance and lack of curiosity"[30] about all worlds beyond our world.

If the misleading certainty of Christianity is to be resisted, so, Montaigne tells us, is the equally suspect hope of logic. The deductive method is all "approaches, definitions, classifications . . . etymologies [and] quarrels . . . over words. . . . A stone is an object. But if you ask: and what is an object?—a substance—and what is a substance? and so on. . . . One [merely] replaces one word with another, that is . . . more complicated and less understood."[31] Such verbal gymnastics are then followed by:

> mixing and chopping . . . small questions [until] the world teem[s] . . . with uncertainty and argument. . . . Have you ever seen [children] trying to divide a mass of quicksilver[32] into a number of parts? The more they press

and squeeze it, and try to control it, the more [it] keeps dividing and spilling into disorder. It's the same here. Engaging in all these subtleties[33] accomplishes little. . . . The purpose of philosophy is to calm us,[34] to teach us . . . virtue, which is not, as the [logicians] say, to be found atop a steep mountain, craggy and hard to climb. Virtue rather resides on a fair, fruitful, and flourishing plateau, with everything visible below. . . . The way to this plateau is by shady, green, and sweetly flowered paths with a pleasant, easy, and smoothly ascending grade. . . . Because they are not familiar with this . . . virtue . . . , which is a professed and implacable enemy to anxiety, fear, sorrow, and constraint, which has nature as her guide and good fortune and pleasure for companions, [logicians] have conjured out of their own weak imaginations their own ridiculous, querulous, unpleasant, spiteful, threatening image of it, and placed it on a rock apart, among thorns and brambles, to frighten people.[35]

Flight from Abstraction

According to Montaigne, what both Christianity and logic share in common is a high level of abstraction, together with a wearisome habit of constantly drawing distinctions and rendering judgments. According to these two great faiths, life is analyzable, generalizable, categorizable, systematizable, simplifiable. Whatever question or problem arises, there is a commandment, a rule, a recipe, a methodology, or a theory to provide guidance. But, protests Montaigne, this is all a pathetic fallacy, a naïve confidence in explanations which on close examination explain nothing.

The truth is that we operate under a veil of ignorance, both in general ("When I play with my cat, is she amusing herself with me, or I with her?")[36] and in the world of value judgments. In addition, the world is ambiguous, full of good that is evil and evil that is good, and "we cannot exist apart from this mixture."[37] Under these circumstances, moral evidence is concrete and personal, not abstract or organizable. Put differently, the proper course of action depends on the particular circumstances, and the best guide is always one's common sense, defined as the ability to hold in one's mind a variety of considerations all at once and then to arrive at a sound and experienced judgment.

Lessons of Sense Experience

The idea that there are no infallible teachers or theories, never have been and never will be, that each of us stands alone and must fashion his or her own destiny, might seem depressing to some. To Montaigne, on the contrary, it would be depressing if answers existed,

◆ Openness to Pleasure

On this point, Montaigne places himself entirely at odds with Christian fundamentalism. He is a man "who accedes to the propensities[44] and desires of his body, who obeys appetites that are insistent," who "hates that inhuman teaching which would make us despise and reject the . . . body,"[45] who places no particular value on monogamy or marital fidelity, and who states that "I have never been harmed by doing anything that was very pleasant[46] for me," although he admits to "a few infections,[47] both minor and fleeting" acquired by unwisely visiting prostitutes. The only real drawback to sexual pleasure as opposed to milder pleasures such as conversation, amusements, books, companionable friends, affection, is that it "withers with age"[48] and, for that very reason, youth should pay no attention to older persons who have been forced into an involuntary repentance. Nor should one try to dress up sex with a spiritual or intellectual fig leaf: "For love is principally a matter of seeing and touching; something can be done without the graces of the mind, nothing without the graces of the body."[49]

◆ Tolerance

To be fully open to sense experience, one must give up the ingrained habit of condemning and criticizing and interfering with others: "I do not inquire if a footman is chaste[50] [nor dismiss as] barbarous anything that is not [my] habit."[51] What is more difficult, one must cultivate a state of mind that actually welcomes criticism from others: "My mind constantly contradicts and condemns. Why should I care if someone else does so? Nor need I give his criticism any more authority than I choose."[52]

◆ Avoidance of Pride, Pretense, Formality, Dishonesty

Such barriers against the world are a particular bane of the middle class, especially the churchgoing middle class. The very rich and very poor often dispense with them, although for quite different reasons (in the one case, complete financial security; in the other, nothing to lose). The middle class is always fearful of revealing itself too fully, of causing offense, and of losing what it has so laboriously accumulated; even so, "it is cowardly and servile to go about in disguise, wearing a mask, without the courage to show oneself as one is. . . .[53] It is not [of course] advisable always to say everything; that would be folly. But we should say what we think." The very worst part of dissimulation and pretense is that it always leads to crippling inner conflict. By being one thing "inside"[54] and another "in front of people," we dissipate our energy and purpose, and lose our ability to "go forward[55] [with] undivided strength."

◆ Avoidance of Rigidity, Eccentricity, Fastidiousness

Inflexibility is a prison to which many of the most independent minds consign themselves. Montaigne himself is not free of this vice, but

> to be ourselves tied and bound of necessity to one [habitual approach] is . . . not to live. . . .[56] The bravest and best souls are pliant and open to variety. . . . [57] A young man needs to toss the rules and give his energy scope. My advice is even to plunge into excess, otherwise any indulgence will overwhelm him and make him a poor companion. The worst quality in a gentleman is over-fastidiousness,[58] too much delicacy, or too much concern about health.[59] . . . I felt I honored a nobleman[60] when I asked him how often he had got drunk while in Germany serving the king. He was glad to respond "three times" and told us some stories.

◆ Avoidance of Obsessions, Ambition, Hard Work, Too Much Seriousness of Purpose

Obsessions are "evil"[61] and an "enemy of life"[62] because they blind a man to all the rich detail and texture of the surrounding world. ("When I walk alone in a beautiful orchard . . . if my thoughts wander to distant events, I bring them back . . . to the walk, the orchard, the pleasure of this solitude.")[63] Ambition is particularly to be avoided, partly because it requires perjuring or obligating or even enslaving oneself to others to gain their support; partly because it is so frequently futile. ("The highest places are usually taken by the worst men. . . .[64] If you do succeed . . . you die[65] and end of story!"); partly because even the most idealistic projects are rarely justified. ("Statilius[66] responded this way when Brutus invited him to join the conspiracy against Caesar; he thought the business just, but did not think that men were worth the trouble."); above all, because it is based on a misapprehension of success:

> "He has wasted his life [on nothing]," we say, and "I have accomplished nothing. . . ." [67] What! Have you not lived? . . . It is great and glorious to live properly. . . . [68] The man who knows how to enjoy his existence has already accomplished everything.[69] We only try for other things, to attain wealth,[70] to create . . . because we do not understand what we are here for, look outside ourselves because we do not understand how to live within ourselves. We can walk on stilts but must rely on our own legs. And if we sit on the mightiest throne,[71] we still sit on our own bottom.

The case against hard work is similar, and just as vehement: "As for pummeling my brain over Aristotle[72] [or putting my] mind . . . on the rack for fourteen or fifteen hours a day,[73] or . . . addicting myself to some area of knowledge[74] . . . that I have not done." Although pure idleness is burdensome and not to be desired, "I am an enemy to constraint, too much work, or too much perseverance." Moreover, the most dangerous hard work is specialized hard work because "our aim should not be to make a grammarian, or a logician, [or any other professional], but a gentleman."[75]

The worst feature of all these worldly obsessions is the way they persist, first in one shape, then in another, always adopting some new and clever disguise. When faced with their blandishments, the only remedy is to check one's seriousness at the door, to reorder one's priorities, to sup at table with "the amusing rather than the wise,"[76] to remember to "choose beauty over goodness . . . in bed," and "for serious conversation [to seek out] liveliness . . . combined with dishonesty."

◆ Detachment

Montaigne's first five virtues "open" a person who might otherwise be "confined and wrapped up"[77] inside. But openness to life is an incomplete virtue; it must be moderated and disciplined in order to prevent a self-destructive orgy of sense experience—of too much sex or other pleasures or a total abandonment of work and ambition—leading to an eventual breakdown. The first and, in some respects, the most important moderating virtue is detachment. More than any other device, it is the ability to watch ourselves from outside, to see ourselves with the same cool impersonal gaze we turn on others, that protects us from an excess of mood or action. Without detachment, we "color"[78] and "quake" from alternating reveries of greed and fear. As proof of his own efforts to achieve detachment, Montaigne attempts to refute the idea that sexual pleasure at its orgasmic peak completely obliterates consciousness. He reports that "it can be otherwise; one can sometimes, by sheer force of will, successfully focus one's mind at that very moment to other thoughts, but one must prepare and make a deliberate effort."[79]

◆ Self-Discipline

In addition to detachment, Montaigne approves of old-fashioned self-discipline. This is not unlike Christian self-discipline in some respects, especially in its underlying assumption about human nature. Whereas most Christians believe in a doctrine of "original sin," that unredeemed human nature is inherently evil and sinful, Montaigne believes that no one, himself included, "is anything but a fool,"[80] a difference more in tone than in substance.

On the other hand, this self-discipline is different. It does not entail dependence, submission, or conformity before a wrathful or loving God; nor deprivation of the flesh; nor the grave and majestic solemnity of ancient puritanism; nor the prim prudery of a bloodless and attenuated puritanism. It is a combination of personal training (thus resurrecting the Greek root of asceticism, which refers to "practice" and, indirectly, to games and sport), of refined good taste, and of ordinary good sense. A mature mind knows that "our desire for [worldly goods] is[81] . . . sharpened by possession rather than scarcity . . . that too much is the enemy of pleasure, that temperance is what truly seasons it."[82] The best precaution to observe is a simple one: Whenever desire becomes insistent, even commanding, pull back. Let a little time pass before indulging that particular appetite again. Montaigne even strikes a metal with the words *Que sais-je* (What do I know?) engraved on one side and *Je m'abstiens* (I restrain myself.) on the other.

◆ Self-Reliance

To strive for self-reliance is yet another way to control oneself. Why? Because self-indulgence, in the form of impatience or too much pleasure or too much ease, invariably involves an imposition on others. When Montaigne faces a variety of worldly dangers, ranging from marauding bandits to court intrigues, he considers seeking help from a more powerful lord. But he quickly realizes "that it [is] safest to count on myself[83] . . . to protect myself, [and so to strengthen myself] that it would take a heavy blow to knock me out of [the] saddle."[84] In this respect, a degree of personal misfortune is a positive good. It hardens us, keeps our passions and weaknesses in check, and helps us to maintain some order and sobriety in the face of limitless temptation.

◆ Eight Virtues in One

Can all eight virtues be summarized in one? One might speak of being simultaneously open and closed; of being a lover but also an athlete of sense experience; of never commanding oneself but always relying on detachment, self-knowledge, and an easy, unserious, good-natured self-discipline; of being in harness, but loose in harness; of being successful and effective without any apparent effort. Although each of these formulations reveals something, they are still entirely too stiff to capture Montaigne's designedly paradoxical doctrine. A picture would be better—a picture, for example, of the younger Scipio, "first among the Romans," who in the midst of planning his fateful military campaign against Hannibal in Africa, a campaign that would decide the future of the civilized world, takes time to "stroll . . . along the seashore, gaily engaged in the childish amusement of picking up and selecting shells, and playing ducks-and-drakes; or, in bad weather entertaining himself with the ribald writing of comedies, in which he reproduce[s] the most ordinary and vulgar actions of men." [85]

Objections to Montaigne

I f one were sitting with Montaigne in his tower, enjoying the kind of civilized conversation he loved, it
would be interesting to learn what he thought about
the following objections to his doctrine of relying on
a highly cultivated and disciplined form of personal
sense experience.

◆ It Is like a Library without a Catalog

According to philosopher Bertrand Russell, Montaigne is "content with confusion; discovery is delightful and system is its enemy."[86] On the surface, this
approach sounds appealing. Do we not learn more
from wonder, search, ambiguity, inconsistency, disorder, paradox, irony, and nuance than from their
opposites? Besides, the rest of Montaigne's arguments
possess an undeniable nobility: that each of us must
find his or her way, with only personal sense experience as a guide; that there are no true authorities, that
dependency is self-destructive, whether on a God or on
another human being; that there are valuable models
to be studied and emulated, but only up to a point, and
only insofar as they fit one's individual case; that one
must immerse oneself in experience, in everyday life,
in books, and in travel, all the while remaining aloof
and detached and forming one's own unique judgment,
taste, and character.

Appealing and noble these doctrines may be, but are they practical? Is a way of life designed by a sixteenth-century gentleman living in a remote corner of France even conceivable today? Since Montaigne's time, many millions of books have been published. The entire world has been opened for travel. Where is one to begin? Should one still regard Horace and Seneca and Plutarch and other ancient Romans as the place to begin in forming and testing one's personal evaluations and beliefs? What about the ancient Greeks? Merely reading the relatively few surviving works of the ancient world, together with all the books written about them, would consume a lifetime, leaving the moderns and all the limitless vistas of travel untouched.

One is reminded of the novelist Thomas Wolfe's gargantuan appetites, of how he tried as an undergraduate at Harvard to read every volume in Widener Library, beginning at random with one stack, and proceeding book by book from there. It is not recorded where Wolfe abandoned the attempt, which was more symbolic than real. The point is that most library users rely on a catalog to guide them, and Montaigne not only eliminates the "catalog"—the direct teaching method of other "religions"—he despises it as an obstacle to our development.

Even Montaigne's literary legacy, the essay form that he invented, tends to thwart the modern student of sense experience. For almost four hundred years, the prestige of the essay, with its charmingly unstructured, digressive, and conversational tone, has been immense. We see it everywhere, in newspapers, magazines, books, or, increasingly, transposed to radio and television. Reporters who have tired of recounting the news like to write short pieces on "loneliness" or "the relations of men and women" or similarly airy topics that mostly serve as a point of departure for unrelated observations or discursive autobiography, and whose contents are often immediately forgettable. The convention of the essay is so strong that even scholarly research articles in some fields are expected to follow the form, to convey new information not just simply and directly and precisely and economically, but with art and indirection. Because few researchers are artists, the result may be only squandered time, both the writer's and the reader's.

◆ It Lacks a Goal or Purpose

In this respect, Montaigne's brand of high sense experience completely denies the basic outlook of the authorities of his day. For example, in Catholicism, even the church, God's representative on earth, is seen as only a means to the ultimate goal of God. In logic, deduction is the means to the goal of an irrefutable argument, a QED (*quod erat demonstrandum*) proof. In high sense experience, sense experience is both the means and the goal. In other words, truth is not something that we find at the end of a quest, it is the quest. This is a revolutionary idea in a purely theoretical sense and in a practical sense as well. Westerners have always been work-and goal-oriented. Yet here is a rather admirable man, Montaigne, who says that the work ethic is misguided; that goals are not important; that one goal, so long as it is disciplined and not an imposition on other people, is about as good as any other; that how you live is more important than what you accomplish.

◆ It Is Selfish

To the observant Christian eye, something else is odd about this ethic of high sense experience. Although it strongly disavows the standard egoistic longings—to reign as a monarch, to win military triumphs, to gain immense riches—it nevertheless glorifies and cultivates the self. *Personal* sense experience, *self*-knowledge, and *self*-control are emphasized to the exclusion of all else, even to the exclusion of unselfish and altruistic acts. Montaigne himself is so likable, so calm, so comfortable, so intimate, that it is easy to overlook this aspect of his doctrine. But it is there all the same, and freely admitted: "I am pleased not to be interested in the affairs of others, and not to be responsible for them."[87] Toward his close friends, the noble seigneur is both protective and loving. Toward his wife and children and servants, he is protective if not particularly loving. Beyond this narrow circle of benevolence there

◆ It Is a Status Symbol

For much of the 1960s and 1970s, high sense experience was anything but a status symbol. The effort to transform it into a mass phenomenon had failed; the PhD glut was a joke; students abandoned art, history, and literature in droves for economics and business courses; art museums and rare book libraries languished. Then, from the 1980s on, something rather unexpected happened. The newly rich, of whom there was an unprecedented supply, especially as the economic bubbles unfolded from the mid-1990s on, began to covet the domestic style and artistic furnishings long associated with people of Montaigne's ilk. The reasons for this phenomenon were complex, but at least one factor was clear. If you had just made millions or billions in a world awash with newly made mega money, money alone would not guarantee social standing or personal prestige. On the other hand, if you owned rare and irreplaceable objects, the kind of objects that Montaigne and others like him had always taken for granted in their households, some of the objects' value and uniqueness might rub off on you.

This transmogrification of high sense experience into high status was at once broadly and narrowly based. It was broadly based in that the newly affluent, often represented by young professional couples, not just the newly rich or newly super-rich, ardently competed as "collectors" or for places on museum committees. Yet it was also narrowly based in that favored objects and institutions had to be suitable for public display, not just private connoisseurship. For example, at the beginning of the twentieth century, truly rare books often sold for more than even the rarest paintings. By the end of the twentieth century, however, rare paintings sold for vastly greater sums, at least partly because they could be displayed on a wall, either in a private residence or in a museum.

A library without a catalog, aimlessness, selfishness, elitism, status seeking: These are harsh charges, and at least partially warranted. It is only fair, however, to listen to a rebuttal, a rebuttal implicitly offered by Joseph Alsop, an American who closely resembled Montaigne in his distinguished lineage, his immense learning and culture, his participation in the public life of his day (as a leading newspaper columnist covering Washington during the post-World War II years of American paramountcy), in his enjoyment of all the civilized and uncivilized pleasures that life has to offer, and not least in the size and frequent use of his library.

Alsop in effect argued that what we call high sense experience in this book has become misunderstood and debased. High sense experience, he said, is simply what the English philosopher and statesman Lord Bolingbroke[88] called "philosophy teaching by examples." The goal of life is to find and follow the example that is right for you; the goal of education is to inculcate a variety of worthy examples from which to choose. Inculcation can be both extensive and luxurious, drawing on huge libraries, comfortable university reading rooms, fine collections and museums, and a long canon of exemplary works; or it can be plain and rough, as plain and rough and non-elitist as Abraham Lincoln educating himself with five or six dog-eared volumes. As Alsop pointed out in the *Washington Post*:

> Lincoln's texts . . . were first of all the Bible and Shakespeare. . . . He not infrequently recited the [Bible] or the great soliloquies, sometimes in the course of important policy discussions, and on a five-hour boat trip to City Point, after Appomattox . . . passed the time for his companions with Shakespeare readings. It is interesting trying to imagine a similar journey by water with one of our last three presidents. After the Bible and Shakespeare, history was his main study. As a young man in New Salem, he read the whole of Gibbon and all of Rollin's history of the world . . . with . . . much space devoted to . . . Greek and Roman history. . . .
>
> The first point that strikes you about the foregoing [list] of books [is that what] Lincoln read and learned is neither read, nor learned, nor even taught in any normal American school or university today. . . .

I do not suppose as many as one university student in a thousand has ever read so much as a chapter of the Bible in the . . . noble . . . King James version, and I fear the same ratio of ignorance prevails among American university professors. . . . If all of us learned to [think and] express ourselves as Lincoln did—by all but getting by heart the King James version—we might even have the cure of the gummy tide of jargon and pseudoscientific pretentiousness which is spreading . . . today.[89]

The Prodigal Alternative to High Sense Experience

High sense experience is composed of one part license and one part discipline, with a garnish of grace and refinement to render the discipline effortless, or at least invisible. Gradually lighten the discipline, eliminate it entirely, or take both license and discipline to fantastic extremes, and you have a very different approach to sense experience, an approach that in Walter Pater's famous phrase seeks "to burn always in [a] hard, gem-like flame, to maintain [an] ecstasy" of experience. Such an approach is no longer the way of Montaigne but rather the way of a prodigal son of Montaigne's, a son who has rebelled against the gentle restraint of the father just as the father rebelled against the severe restraint of Catholic Christianity.

This basic intergenerational quarrel between two related but very different doctrines, each based on sense experience but drawing quite different conclusions, may be illustrated by an episode from Thomas Merton's memoirs, *The Seven Storey Mountain*. Both of Merton's parents had died, and while he was studying at an English secondary school, his godfather, a fashionable English doctor and an old friend of his father's, offered his London flat to Merton as a refuge during school holidays. The flat was luxurious, with beautiful antiques, a French maid, and every comfort, including breakfast in bed. Conversation at the dinner table or later over coffee in the drawing room was sophisticated, witty, worldly, derisory of Christianity and middle-class morals, preoccupied with new art, films, books, or the latest word on which English aristocrat was "thought to take dope." Tom breathed in this atmosphere like the purest oxygen and began to imitate his godfather's every taste and mannerism. Yet when he began to squander his allowance and got a girlfriend pregnant, this led to an irreparable breach: it was one thing to be free in conversation, quite another to be free in conduct. For as Montaigne had said, a gentleman might be "disordered," "unrestrained," even "depraved" in his "opinions," but not "imprudent" in his "appetites."[90]

Merton did not long remain a prodigal son. By embracing the Roman Catholic Church and becoming a Trappist monk in Kentucky, he repudiated a religion of sense experience entirely, both his godfather's high version and his own wilder version. In any case, it is doubtful whether Merton was ever a complete prodigal because, although he was always attracted to rebellion, escapism, and fantasy, he never completely gave himself up to a biblical "wasting of substance." To be a complete prodigal, one must be determined to affront the comfortable; to defy the respectable; to abjure "maturity" and "responsibility"; to repudiate seriousness, caution, decency, normalcy, and wholesomeness; to avoid a "normal" career, raising children, or participating in politics; to be rebellious and insolent, yet playful and lighthearted; full of brilliance, wit, extravagance, and surprise; capable of shocking, dazzling, and charming all at once—in short, to retain all the superficial ease and polish and verve of the high religion of sense experience without any of the character building that is supposed to take place beneath the surface.

Although the traits just enumerated describe a similar approach to sense experience, there is no single, uniform way of life among prodigals. Even more than with high sense experience, which already abhors systematization or generalization, prodigality must be approached through specific individuals, all of whom are rebels, escapists, and fantasists, but who differ sharply in interpretation and degree. Only by separately scrutinizing their lives, beginning with the romantic escapism of the novelist Lawrence Durrell and ending with the profligacy of the playwright Tennessee Williams, is it possible to build up a collective portrait, to define the faith in concrete terms, to decide what prodigality really means, both for those who adopt it and for those who must live with those who adopt it.

The Romantic Escapist

At age twenty-three, poet and novelist Lawrence Durrell abandons industrial society "as serene and bland as suet . . . which dispossessed me of myself and tried to destroy in me all that was singular and unique."[91] With one completed novel, a new wife, and a $20 per week allowance from his mother, he sets out for the Greek island of Corfu, a verdant gem set in the blue Ionian Sea ("Somewhere between Calabria and Corfu the blue really begins") and discovers a world of sun, land, and seascape, friends, work, love, physical pleasure, tastes, sounds, sights, smells, touch; a world of pure happiness, protectively bracketed against the intrusion of past or future. The description that follows is taken from a diary, kept between

April 1937 and September 1938, later incorporated into *Prospero's Cell*:

5.5.37

The books have arrived by water. Confusion, adjectives, smoke, and the deafening pumping of the wheezy Diesel engine. . . .

4.7.37

We breakfast at sunrise after a bathe. Grapes and Hymettos honey, black coffee, eggs, and the light clear-tasting Papastratos cigarette. Unconscious transition from the balcony to the rock outside. . . . Sitting here on this spit we can see the dolphins and the steamers passing within hail almost. We bathe naked, and the sun and water make our skins feel old and rough, like precious lace.[92]

The Naïf

If an island idyll in the Mediterranean represents one kind of rebellion, escape, and fantasy, another is simple naïveté, a childlike refusal to face the realities of adult life, as exemplified by Lawrence Durrell's description of his good friend and mentor, the novelist Henry Miller:[93]

As for Henry, he was never there; he was always lost in his dreams. One day he even had the idea of taking a train to Berlin, so as to go and talk to Hitler for five minutes to persuade him to abandon his military ambitions!

The Aesthete

For the aesthete, rebellion, escapism, and fantasy are closely allied with a larger agenda of beauty and taste. To live well is to surround oneself and devote oneself to *objets d'art* and *objets de luxe*. At its worst, this approach is everything that Montaigne dislikes: a kind of hot-house "ladies-and-gents" mentality, that is, a passive and conspicuous fastidiousness, an elaborately self-conscious ritual of choosing the right wines, clothes, and interior decoration.

Yet as the British-American writer Harold Acton[94] demonstrates, aestheticism has a positive dimension as well, a dimension of genuine appreciation, style, and erudition. In Acton's case, the style is cosmopolitan and gently nostalgic, reflecting passage through a variety of dying worlds, beginning (and ending) with a Florentine *palazzo*, but encompassing prewar Eton and Oxford, prewar China, southern Italy, and America:

> In 1936 I celebrated the twenty-fifth anniversary of the Chinese Republic by moving

into a perfect [Peking] mansion, with three successive courtyards and a side garden. . . .

Here I had ample space to hang all my pictures and arrange the old furniture I had collected. . . .

Thrust out of China by war and the Communist revolution, Acton turns his attention to the fading Bourbon aristocracy of Southern Italy:

The Princess of Trabia held a formal court of abbes who still took snuff. . . . Unfortunately I had no leisure to browse in the library which contained many rare tomes I longed to read.

A few years later, Acton visited his mother's closest friend, Florence Crane,[95] who lived at "Castle Hill" on Boston's North Shore (the Massachusetts coast above Boston). The original structure on the site had been built by Mr. Crane as a surprise for his bride. When he asked how she liked it, she had responded, "I don't like one thing about it," and had then demolished it and built a "more classical residence of pink brick imported from Holland."

[The new mansion] was splendidly furnished in Queen Anne style, seven of the fifty-two rooms with paneling from Hogarth's London house. . . . The sporting and marine paintings interested me less, but I coveted Zoffany's portrait of Lunardi the Balloonist at Windsor. Sumptuous editions of the classics gleamed on the shelves of the library transported from Essex House.

[Mrs. Crane and her friends] were devoted gardeners. . . . Having sublimated or eliminated what is now generically called sex, they had settled down to cultivate "gracious living."

The Decadent

A 1983 photo in *W* (the glossy periodical offshoot of the fashion newspaper *Women's Wear Daily*) shows a tall, thin, mustachioed man standing beside various Art Deco objects in his house. The caption reads:

It's inappropriate to call Richard Nelson,[96] creative director of Neiman Marcus advertising, a collector of Art Deco. It's his entire life style, from the vintage Howard Hughestype printed sportshirts and pleated pants he finds in thrift shops to his 1936 Deco house, complete with a 1949 DeSoto in the garage.

"My favorite moments come when I fill the house with old records of Dick Powell and Fred Astaire, invite a few friends over, and forget

we're living now. My mother and father were
like Ozzie and Harriet; and my name's Nelson, so I grew up with apple pie," he reflects.
"Maybe that's why I want to be decadent."

As Nelson implies, decadence involves something
more than a combination of rebellion, escapism,
and aestheticism. It looks backward, toward an ide-
alized and irrecoverable past. As French couturier
Yves Saint Laurent[97] says: "People think decadence
is debauched. Decadence is simply something very
beautiful that is [dead or] dying." It is also quintes-
sentially passive in its attitudes. Ironically, decadents
may be the very reverse of prodigal libertines: they
may lead forgotten, hidden, covered-up lives with little travel, a routine job, few friends, few adventures,
few beautiful objects. Yet pleasure and experience are
still their gods, and the very sparseness of their existence, the unbridgeable distance that separates them
from the past they crave creates a kind of burning
emotional intensity. The idea of loss, of love affairs
living only in memory, of objects that might have
been possessed but that are snatched away by a capri-
cious and ungovernable fate, kindles the imagination
and transmutes vanity, corruption, disillusion, cyni-
cism, pretense, depravity, vice, self-deception, paraly-
sis, fear, and irresolution, all the weary weakness of
the flesh, into the highest and most esoteric form of
art. Constantine Cavafy,[98] one of Lawrence Durrell's

favorite poets, the aging Alexandrian waterworks official who lived in a tiny upstairs flat in Alexandria, wrote in "One Night":

> The bedroom was cheap, vulgar
> secret over a dubious bar.
> From the window you'd see the alley
> dirty and narrow.
> Some working-hands' voices
> came up from below.
> They were playing cards
>
> and having a party.
> There in that common, low-class bed
> I had love's body, I had the lips
> voluptuous and rosy red of drunken rapture
> rosy red of such a drunken rapture
> that now as I write—after so many years—
> in my house by myself
> I am drunk with rapture again.

The Profligate

At the end of the downward spiral, with self-discipline positively scorned,* are the sexual and hallucinatory experiences of the playwright Tennessee Williams, as described in his *Memoirs*:

---

* One thinks of a remark by the French author and film director (and quintessential prodigal) Jean Cocteau: "The tact of audacity consists in knowing how far to go too far."

> The other night I was feeling lively, so we
> took to the streets, here in New Orleans.[99]
> I whispered to my companion that I was "in
> heat," so we went again to that delightfully
> scandalous night spot on Bourbon Street
> which features the topless and bottomless....

Some time later, Williams describes a television interview in which he berates Richard Nixon for his "lack of . . . a moral sense." This, in turn, reminds him of another incident:

> On the subject of television shows, I was
> living, at a point in the sixties . . . in New
> York City.[100] I was at that time under drugs,
> rather deeply, and did not know . . . that I
> had previously acquiesced . . . to a request by
> the TV commentator Mike Wallace to in-
> terview me in my apartment that morning.
>
> Out I came stumbling in a pair of shorts
> from my bedroom.... I entered the blaze of
> television cameras.... A full TV crew had
> been set up.... I fell down flat on my face.

Based on the foregoing, it is obvious that prodigals share much in common. Although some carry both self-discipline *and* license to exaggerated extremes (treks to the North Pole followed by wild bouts of sexual promiscuity) and others are spurred by at least one of the three

It is now time for me to consider the question of whether or not I am a lunatic or a relatively sane person....[102] I say *non contendere*.... Most of you belong to something that offers a stabilizing influence: a family unit, a defined social position, employment in an organization.... I am a fugitive.... [But] if you can't be yourself, what's the point of being anything at all?[103]

Note regarding the quoted material used in this chapter:
Essays, translation by Hunter Lewis.

Chapter 8

Baruch de Spinoza

(1632–1677)

S PINOZA'S LIFE, AS well as his doctrines, reflects the possibilities of a pure "religion" of deductive logic, where "religion" is defined as a set of personal evaluations and beliefs and actions inspired by those evaluations and beliefs, not just a socially organized religion like Judaism or Christianity. A solitary bachelor, Spinoza moved from town to town to escape the time-consuming attentions of his devoted friends; an imperturbable boarder, he sometimes remained in his room for three months at a time, to the fond amazement of whatever family he was staying with; an expert lens grinder, he always paid his own way and gently declined the financial patronage of princes. As Spinoza

explained the motive behind this unconventional existence, which some of his contemporaries viewed as a
kind of extreme secular monasticism:

> After experience had taught me that all the
> usual surroundings of social life are vain
> and futile, and seeing that none of the ob-
> jects of my fears contained in themselves
> anything either good or bad, except inso-
> far as the mind is affected by them, I finally
> resolved to inquire whether there might be
> some real good having power to commu-
> nicate itself, which would affect the mind
> singly, to the exclusion of all else—whether,
> in fact, there might be anything of which
> the discovery and attainment would en-
> able me to enjoy continuous, supreme,
> and unending happiness.

> I say "I *finally* resolved," for at first sight it
> seemed unwise willingly to lose hold on what
> was sure for the sake of something then un-
> certain. I could see the benefits which are
> acquired through fame and riches, and that
> I should be obliged to abandon the quest of
> such objects, if I seriously devoted myself to
> the search for something different and new.
> I perceived that if true happiness chanced to
> be placed in the former I should necessarily

miss it; while if, on the other hand, it were not so placed, and I gave them my whole attention, I should equally fail.

I therefore debated whether it would not be possible to arrive at the new principle or at any rate at a certainty concerning its existence, without changing the conduct and usual plan of my life. With this end in view I made many efforts, but in vain. . . .

For the ordinary surroundings of life which are esteemed by men (as their actions testify) to be the highest good may be classed under the three heads—Riches, Fame, and the Pleasures of Sense: with these three the mind is so absorbed that it has little power to reflect on any different good. By sensual pleasure the mind is enthralled . . . so that it is quite incapable of thinking of any other object; when such pleasure has been gratified it is followed by extreme melancholy. The pursuit of honors and riches is likewise very absorbing, especially if such objects be sought simply for their own sake. . . . In the case of fame the mind is still more absorbed, for fame is conceived as always good for its own sake, and as the ultimate end to which all actions are directed. Further the attainment of riches and fame is not followed as in the case of sensual pleasure by repentance, but, the more we acquire, the greater is our delight, and consequently, the more we are incited to increase both the one and the other; on the other hand, if our hopes happen to be frustrated, we are plunged into the deepest sadness. Fame has the further drawback that it compels its votaries to order their lives according to the opinions of their fellow men, shunning what they usually shun, and seeking what they usually seek.

When I saw that all these ordinary objects of desire would be obstacles in the way of a search for something different and new— no, that they were so opposed thereto that either they or it would have to be abandoned, I was forced to inquire which would prove the most useful to me. But further reflection convinced me that . . . evils arise from the love of what is perishable, such as the objects already mentioned [while] love toward a thing eternal and infinite feeds the mind wholly with joy, and is itself unmingled with any sadness, wherefore it is greatly to be desired and sought for with all our strength.

> [Even then] I could not forthwith lay aside
> all love of riches, sensual enjoyment, and
> fame. [But] while my mind was employed
> with [deductive logic], it turned away from
> its former objects of desire. . . . Although
> these intervals were at first rare, and of very
> short duration, yet afterwards, . . . they be-
> came more frequent and more lasting. (*On
> the Improvement of the Understanding*)

After persevering in this highly disciplined existence for many years, Spinoza concluded that the all-
important initial premise, the logical key that would
unlock a complete system of values, could be found in
the concept of perfection. For perfection to be truly
perfect it must be absolute; and to be absolute, it must
exist. From this *a priori* argument (*a priori* because it is
thought to be self-evidently true), one may infer that
God (another name for perfection) must exist, and one
may then proceed, step by step, through definitions,
axioms, and propositions laid out like Euclid's geom-
etry, to a complete cosmological and ethical system.

Like Spinoza's modest life of humility and retirement,
the Spinozan philosophical system might seem super-
ficially compatible with traditional Jewish or Christian
belief: It places God at the beginning of the reasoning chain. But unlike systems based on the cosmological argument for the existence of God (the observable
phenomenon of cause and effect in the universe implies

God as a First Cause) or the teleological argument (the organization of the universe implies God as an initial Organizer), Spinoza's ontological argument (to be perfect, God must be) does not necessarily assume a God like that of Judaism or Christianity. Indeed, Spinoza concluded that God was more likely to be the universe (pantheism) than the creator of the universe (theism), and this position led to excommunication from his synagogue, near assassination, and dismissal by a Christian acquaintance as a "wretched little man, [a] vile worm of the earth."

Eventually, Spinoza's ontological argument, together with its cosmological and teleological counterparts, was refuted by other philosophers, notably David Hume and Immanuel Kant in the eighteenth century. Thereafter, these logical set pieces lived a kind of half-life, appearing and reappearing, revived, re-refuted, revived again. Even in the 1980s, some contemporary American scientists speculated about an "anthropic principle" that bears a close resemblance to the cosmological and teleological arguments, and toward the end of his life, Einstein insisted, "I believe in Spinoza's God." Meanwhile Spinoza's attitude, as opposed to his precise logical technique, has never lost its power to move. As Goethe wrote:

> After I had looked around the whole world
> in vain for a means of developing my strange
> nature, I finally hit upon the *Ethics* of this
> man. . . . Here I found the serenity to calm

my passions; a wide and free view over the
material and moral world seemed to open
before me. Above all, I was fascinated by the
boundless disinterestedness that emanated
from him. That wonderful sentence "He
who truly loves God must not desire God
to love him in return" with all the propositions on which it rests, with all the consequences that spring from it, filled my whole
subsequent thought.

Note regarding the quoted material used in this chapter:

On the Improvement of the Understanding by Baruch de Spinoza, an
updated version of translation by R. H. M. Elwes.

Chapter 9

David Hume

(1711–1776)

Part One: Religion

IF ANYBODY QUALIFIES as a secular saint, it must surely be Scottish philosopher David Hume. Secular certainly describes him: he regarded religion as the supreme source of both superstition and fanaticism, the twin evils which bedeviled and enslaved the human mind.

That he was saint-like in his personal life may be more arguable, but there is plenty of evidence for it. Here is Hume's description of himself, an account that was verified by everyone who knew him:

> . . . I possess the same ardor as ever in study,
> and the same gaiety in company. . . . It is dif-
> ficult to be more detached from life than I
> am at present. . . .

> . . . I was, I say, a man of mild dispositions,
> of command of temper, of an open, social,
> and cheerful humor, capable of attachment,
> but little susceptible of enmity, and of great
> moderation in all my passions. . . . ("My
> Own Life")

His close friend Adam Smith, the great economist,
witnessed his stoic and uncomplaining acceptance of
death, as diarrhea steadily robbed him of strength, and
on his passing wrote the following to Hume's publisher
and friend William Strahan:

> Thus died our most excellent, and never to
> be forgotten friend; concerning whose . . .
> character and conduct there can scarce be a
> difference of opinion. His temper, indeed,
> seemed to be more happily balanced, if I
> may be allowed such an expression, than
> that perhaps of any other man I have ever
> known. . . . The extreme gentleness of his
> nature never weakened . . . the steadiness
> of his resolutions. His constant pleasantry
> was the genuine effusion of good-nature
> and good-humor, tempered with delicacy

and modesty, and without even the slightest tincture of malignity.... Upon the whole, I have always considered him, both in his lifetime and since his death, as approaching as nearly to the idea of a perfectly wise and virtuous man, as perhaps the nature of human frailty will permit. (Letter from Adam Smith to William Strahan)

As amiable, lovable, and serene as Hume always seemed to appear to his friends, he was also fully human. This is how the youthful Hume described himself in his first book:

> ... I have exposed myself to the enmity of all metaphysicians, logicians, mathematicians, and even theologians.... When I look abroad, I foresee on every side, dispute, contradiction, anger, calumny and detraction. When I turn my eye inward, I find nothing but doubt and ignorance....

> Most fortunately it happens, that since reason is incapable of dispelling these clouds, nature herself suffices to that purpose, and cures me of this philosophical melancholy and delirium, either by relaxing this bent of mind, or by some avocation, and lively impression of my senses, which obliterate all these chimeras. I dine, I play a game of

backgammon, I converse, and am merry
with my friends. . . .

[Even so], I make bold to recommend philosophy, and shall not scruple to give it the
preference to superstition of every kind or
denomination. . . . The [ancient Greek] Cyn-
ics are an extraordinary instance of philosophers, who from reasonings purely philosophical ran into as great extravagancies of
conduct as any Monk or Dervish that ever
was in the world. Generally speaking, the
errors in religion are dangerous; those in
philosophy only ridiculous.

I am sensible, that . . . there are in England,
in particular, many honest gentlemen, who
being always employed in their domestic
affairs, or amusing themselves in common
recreations, have carried their thoughts very
little beyond those objects, which are every
day exposed to their senses. And indeed, of
such as these I pretend not to make philosophers. . . . They do well to keep themselves
in their present situation; and instead of
refining them into philosophers, I wish we
could communicate to our founders of systems, a share of this gross earthy mixture, as
an ingredient, which they commonly stand

> much in need of. . . . (*A Treatise of Human Nature*, Book I, Section VII)

This reflective, learned, cultivated, gentle, tolerant, calm, companionable, loyal, witty, and good man was also an implacable foe of all religion, which he considered an evil. In a letter to a friend, he referred to the realm of "Stupidity, Christianity, and Ignorance." (Hume to Hugh Blair, April 6, 1765)

Peter Gay, in his superb, two-volume history of the European "Enlightenment" movement of Hume's time, mentions this letter (vol. 1, p. 20). He also recounts (vol. 1, p. 356–57) how James Boswell, Samuel Johnson's celebrated biographer and a firm Christian believer, despite his acknowledged moral lapses, visited Hume on his deathbed in a last effort to save his soul. He found Hume "lean, ghastly, and quite of an earthy appearance." When Boswell asked whether "it was not possible there might be a future state," the philosopher responded that "it was a most unreasonable fancy that he should exist forever." Boswell, thinking of "my excellent mother's pious instructions," then asked "would it not be agreeable to have hopes of seeing our friends again?" and "mentioned three men lately deceased, for whom I knew he had a high value." Hume "owned that it would be agreeable, but added that none of them entertained such a notion. I believe he said, such a foolish, or such an absurd notion. . . ." This final interview was entirely consistent with the way Hume led his entire life. The foe of Christianity, whose own personal life had been so exemplary, faced extinction with unwavering calm and courage.

Here follows a summary of his thoughts on religion:

1. Of Theology

> ... [The work] ... of [theologians] ... arise[s] either from ... human vanity ..., or from the craft of popular superstitions.... Chased from the open country ... [of reason], these robbers fly into the forest, and lie in wait to break in upon every unguarded avenue of the mind, and overwhelm it with religious fears and prejudices.... (*An Enquiry Concerning Human Understanding*, Section I, 6)

2. Of Miracles

> ... As the evidence, derived from witnesses and human testimony, is founded on past experience, so it varies with the experience, and is regarded either as a *proof* or a *probability*.... The ultimate standard, by which we determine all disputes, that may arise concerning them, is always derived from experience and observation....

A miracle is a violation of the laws of nature; ... There must ... be a uniform experience against every miraculous event, otherwise the event would not merit that appellation. And as a uniform experience amounts to a proof, there is here a direct and full *proof*, from the nature of the fact, against the existence of any miracle; nor can such a proof be destroyed, or the miracle rendered credible, but by an opposite proof, which is superior.

The plain consequence is (and it is a general maxim worthy of our attention), "That no testimony is sufficient to establish a miracle, unless the testimony be of such a kind, that its falsehood would be more miraculous, than the fact, which it endeavors to establish...." (Ibid., Section X, Part I)

It is easy to show, that ... there never was a miraculous event established on so full an evidence.... In addition, we observe ... that ... whatever is different is contrary; ... all the prodigies of different religions are to be regarded as contrary facts, and the evidences of these prodigies, whether weak or strong, as opposite to each other.... This argument ... is not in reality different from

the reasoning of a judge, who supposes, that
the credit of two witnesses, maintaining a
crime against any one, is destroyed by the
testimony of two others. . . .

. . . Let us [now] examine those miracles, related in scripture; and not to lose ourselves
in too wide a field, . . . confine ourselves to
such as we find in the *Pentateuch*. . . . Here . . .
we . . . consider a book, presented to us by a
barbarous and ignorant people, . . . and in
all probability long after the facts which it
relates, corroborated by no concurring testimony. . . . Upon reading this book, we find
it full of prodigies and miracles. It gives an
account of a state of the world and of human nature entirely different from the present: of our fall from that state; of the age
of man, extended to near a thousand years;
of the destruction of the world by a del-
uge; of the arbitrary choice of one people,
as the favorites of heaven; and that people
the countrymen of the author; of their de-
liverance from bondage by prodigies the
most astonishing imaginable. I desire any
one to lay his hand upon his heart, and after a serious consideration declare, whether
he thinks that the falsehood of such a book,
supported by such a testimony, would be

more extraordinary and miraculous than all the miracles it relates. . . .

We may conclude [from this], that the *Christian Religion* not only was at first attended with miracles, but even at this day cannot be believed by any reasonable person without one. Mere reason is insufficient to convince us of its veracity: and whoever is moved by *Faith* to assent to it, is conscious of a continued miracle in his own person, which subverts all the principles of his understanding, and gives him a determination to believe what is most contrary to custom and experience. (Ibid., Section X, Part II)

3. Of Religious Behavior

Celibacy, fasting, penance, mortification, self-denial, humility, silence, solitude, and the whole train of monkish virtues; for what reason are they everywhere rejected by men of sense, but because they serve no manner of purpose; neither advance a man's fortune in the world, nor render him a more valuable member of society; neither qualify him for the entertainment of company, nor increase his power of self-enjoyment? We observe, on the contrary, that they cross

all these desirable ends; stupefy the understanding and harden the heart, obscure the
fancy and sour the temper. We justly, therefore, transfer them to the opposite column,
and place them in the catalog of vices; nor
has any superstition force sufficient among
men of the world, to pervert entirely these
natural sentiments. A gloomy, hair-brained
enthusiast, after his death, may have a place
in the calendar; but will scarcely ever be admitted, when alive, into intimacy and society, except by those who are as delirious and
dismal as himself. (*An Enquiry Concerning
the Principles of Morals*, Section IX, Conclusion, Part I)

4. Philosophy as an Antidote to Religion

Philosophy . . . is . . . the sovereign antidote
to . . . superstition and false religion. All other
remedies against that pestilent distemper are
vain, or, at least, uncertain. Plain good sense
and the practice of the world, which alone
serve most purposes of life, are here found
ineffectual: History, as well as daily experience, affords instances of men, endowed with
the strongest capacity for business and affairs,
who have all their lives crouched under slavery to the grossest superstition. Even gaiety

and sweetness of temper, which infuse a balm into every other wound, afford no remedy to so virulent a poison. . . . But when sound philosophy has once gained possession of the mind, superstition is effectually excluded; and one may safely affirm, that her triumph over this enemy is more complete than over most of the vices and imperfections, incident to human nature. Love or anger, ambition or avarice, have their root in the temper and affections, which the soundest reason is scarce ever able fully to correct. But superstition, being founded on false opinion, must immediately vanish, when true philosophy has inspired juster sentiments of superior powers. . . .

It will here be superfluous to magnify the merits of philosophy, by displaying the pernicious tendency of that vice, of which it cures the human mind. The superstitious man, says Tully [Cicero], is miserable in every scene, in every incident of life. Even sleep itself, which banishes all other cares of unhappy mortals, affords to him matter of new terror; while he examines his dreams, and finds in those visions of the night, prognostications of future calamities. ("On Suicide")

5. Of Superstition and Enthusiasm

These two species of false religion, though both pernicious, are yet of a very different, and even of a contrary nature. The mind of man is subject to certain unaccountable terrors and apprehensions.... As these enemies are entirely invisible and unknown, the methods taken to appease them are equally unaccountable, and consist in ceremonies, observances, mortifications, sacrifices, presents, or in any practice, however absurd or frivolous, which either folly or knavery recommends to a blind and terrified credulity....

But the mind of man is also subject to an unaccountable elevation and presumption.... In such a state of mind, the imagination swells with great, but confused conceptions, to which no sublunary beauties or enjoyments can correspond. Everything mortal and perishable vanishes as unworthy of attention; and a full range is given to the fancy in the invisible regions, or world of Spirits.... Hence arise raptures, transports, and surprising flights of fancy; and, confidence and presumption still increasing, these raptures, being altogether unaccountable, and seeming quite beyond the reach of our ordinary faculties, are attributed to the immediate inspiration of that Divine Being who is the object of devotion. In a little time, the inspired person comes to regard himself as a distinguished favorite of the Divinity; and when this frenzy once takes place, ... the fanatic madman delivers himself over ... to inspiration from above. ...

Religions which partake of enthusiasm, are, on their first rise, more furious and violent than those which partake of superstition; but in a little time become more gentle and moderate.... Enthusiasm produces the most cruel disorders in human society; but its fury is like that of thunder and tempest, which exhaust themselves in a little time, and leave the air more calm and serene than before.... Superstition, on the contrary, steals in gradually and insensibly; renders men tame and submissive; is acceptable to the magistrate, and seems inoffensive to the people; till at last the priest, having firmly established his authority, becomes the tyrant and disturber of human society, by his endless contentions, persecutions, and religious wars. ...

Superstition is [also] an enemy to civil liberty, and enthusiasm a friend to it. As superstition groans under the dominion of priests, and enthusiasm is destructive of all ecclesiastical power, this sufficiently accounts for the present observation. Not to mention that enthusiasm, being the infirmity of bold and ambitious tempers, is naturally accompanied with a spirit of liberty; as superstition, on the contrary, renders men tame and abject, and fits them for slavery.... ("Of Superstition and Enthusiasm")

6. Of an Afterlife

... There arise ... in some minds ... unaccountable terrors with regard to futurity; but these would quickly vanish were they not artificially fostered by precept and education. And those who foster them, what is their motive? Only to gain a livelihood, and to acquire power and riches in this world. Their very zeal and industry, therefore, are an argument against them.

What cruelty, what iniquity, what injustice in nature, to confine all our concern, as well as all our knowledge, to the present life, if there be another scene still waiting us of infinitely greater consequence? Ought this barbarous deceit to be ascribed to a beneficent and wise being? ...

Punishment, according to *our* conception, should bear some proportion to the offense. Why then eternal punishment for the temporary offenses of so frail a creature as man?...
Heaven and hell suppose two distinct species of men, the good and the bad; but the greatest part of mankind float betwixt vice and virtue....

The chief source of moral ideas is the reflection on the interests of human society. Ought these interests, so short, so frivolous, to be guarded by punishments eternal and infinite?...

Nature has rendered human infancy peculiarly frail and mortal, as it were on purpose to refute the notion of a probationary state; the half of mankind die before they are rational creatures....

Nothing in this world is perpetual; everything, however seemingly firm, is in continual flux and change: The world itself gives symptoms of frailty and dissolution. How contrary to analogy, therefore, to imagine that one single [human] form, seeming the frailest of any, and subject to the greatest disorders, is immortal and indissoluble? What theory is that! How lightly, not to say how rashly, entertained!...

How to dispose of the infinite number of [deceased persons] ought also to embarrass the religious theory. Every planet in every solar system, we are at liberty to imagine peopled with intelligent mortal beings, at least we can fix on no other supposition. For these then a new universe must every generation be created . . . to admit of this continual influx of beings. . . .

. . . Death is in the end unavoidable. . . . All doctrines are to be suspected which are favored by our passions; and the hopes and fears which gave rise to this doctrine are very obvious. . . . ("On the Immortality of the Soul")

7. Whence Religion?

. . . As the *causes* which bestow happiness or misery are, in general, very little known and very uncertain, our anxious concern endeavors to attain a determinate idea of them, and finds no better expedient than to represent them as intelligent, voluntary agents, like ourselves; only somewhat superior in power and wisdom. . . . (*The Natural History of Religion*, Section V)

. . . Rather than relinquish this propensity to adulation, religionists in all ages have involved themselves in the greatest absurdities and contradictions. (Ibid., Section VI)

8. Paganism Is in Some Respects Superior to Christian Monotheism

... The tolerating spirit of idolaters, both in ancient and modern times, is very obvious to anyone who is the least conversant in the writings of historians or travelers. When the oracle of Delphi was asked, what rites or worship was most acceptable to the Gods? "Those legally established in each city," replied the oracle. ...

... So sociable is polytheism, that the utmost fierceness and aversion which it meets with in an opposite religion is scarcely able to disgust it, and keep it at a distance. Augustus praised extremely the reserve of his grandson, Caius Caesar, when this latter prince, passing by Jerusalem, deigned not to sacrifice according to the Jewish law. But for what reason did Augustus so much approve of this conduct? Only because that religion was by the Pagans esteemed ignoble and barbarous. ... (Ibid., Section IX)

... Where the deity is represented as infinitely superior to mankind, this belief, ... is apt, when joined with superstitious terrors, to sink the human mind into the lowest submission and abasement, and to represent the monkish virtues of mortification, penance, humility, and passive suffering, as the only qualities which are acceptable to him. . . .

Bellarmine patiently and humbly allowed the fleas and other odious vermin to prey upon him. "We shall have heaven," said he, "to reward us for our sufferings; but these poor creatures have nothing but the enjoyment of the present life." Such difference is there between the maxims of a Greek hero and a Catholic saint. (Ibid., Section X)

9. Christianity, Even More than Other Religions, Should Be Regarded as Absurd

. . . It must be allowed that the Roman Catholics are a very learned sect, and that no one communion but that of the Church of England can dispute their being the most learned of all the Christian Churches. Yet Averroes, the famous Arabian, who, no doubt, has heard of the Egyptian superstitions, declares that of all religions the most absurd and nonsensical is that whose votaries eat, after having created, their deity. . . . (Ibid., Section XII)

10. Religion Also Brings Unintended Consequences

... In life ... good and ill are universally intermingled and confounded; happiness and misery, wisdom and folly, virtue and vice. Nothing is purely and entirely of a piece. All advantages are attended with disadvantages. . . . The more exquisite any good is, of which a small specimen is afforded us, the sharper is the evil allied to it; and few exceptions are found to this uniform law of nature. . . . As the good, the great, the sublime, the ravishing, are found eminently in the genuine principles of theism; it may be expected, from the analogy of nature, that the base, the absurd, the mean, the terrifying, will be discovered equally in religious fictions and chimeras. . . .

Survey most nations and most ages. Examine the religious principles which have, in fact, prevailed in the world. You will scarcely be persuaded that they are other than sick men's dreams. . . . [There are] no theological absurdities so glaring as have not, sometimes, been embraced by men of the greatest and most cultivated understanding. No religious precepts so rigorous as have not been adopted by the most voluptuous and most abandoned of men.... What so pure as some of the morals included in some theological systems? What so corrupt as some of the practices to which these systems give rise?

The comfortable views exhibited by the belief of futurity are ravishing and delightful. But how quickly they vanish on the appearance of its terrors, which keep a more firm and durable possession of the human mind! (Ibid., Section XV)

11. It Is Best to Escape This Realm of "Fury and Contention"

The whole is a riddle, an enigma, an inexplicable mystery. Doubt, uncertainty, suspense of judgment, appear the only result of our most accurate scrutiny concerning this subject. But such is the frailty of human reason, and such the irresistible contagion of opinion, that even this deliberate doubt could scarcely be upheld, did we not enlarge our view, and, opposing one species of superstition to another, set them a quarrelling; while we ourselves, during their fury and contention, happily make our escape into the calm, though obscure, regions of philosophy. (Ibid.)

12. Traditional Philosophical Arguments for the Existence of God Are Flawed

What follows, is taken from the *Dialogues Concerning Natural Religion*, written in 1751, but held back from publication because of its controversial nature until 1779, three years after Hume's death. This work presents a debate between three fictional characters:

- **PHILO**, a skeptical philosopher who believes conventional religion does more harm than good;

- **CLEANTHES**, who wants to reconcile Christian faith and reason, who bases his arguments on experience alone, and who rejects logical proofs of God's existence, and;

- **DEMEA**, a traditional Christian whose religion is based on faith, but who also accepts logical proofs of God's existence.

It is believed that Philo speaks for Hume both in general and in the famous refutations of the philosophical "proofs" for God's existence, the argument from design (the world shows the handiwork of a master designer) and the ontological argument (to be perfect, God must be).

PHILO (skeptic):

" . . . Let us become thoroughly sensible of the weakness, blindness, and narrow limits of human reason; let us duly consider its

so much insisted on by philosophers, all fallacy, all sophism? Can we reach no further in this subject than experience and probability? I will not say that this is betraying the cause of a Deity: but surely . . . you give advantages to Atheists. . . ."

PHILO (skeptic):

"What I chiefly scruple in this subject," said Philo, "is not so much that all religious arguments are by Cleanthes reduced to experience, as that they appear not to be even the most certain and irrefragable of that inferior kind. That a stone will fall, that fire will burn, that the earth has solidity, we have observed a thousand and a thousand times; and when any new instance of this nature is presented, we draw without hesitation the accustomed inference. The exact similarity of the cases gives us a perfect assurance of a similar event; and a stronger evidence is never desired nor sought after. But wherever you depart, in the least, from the similarity of the cases, you diminish proportionally the evidence; and may at last bring it to a very weak analogy, which is confessedly liable to error and uncertainty. . . .

"If we see a house, Cleanthes, we conclude, with the greatest certainty, that it had an architect or builder because this is precisely that species of effect which we have experienced to proceed from that species of cause. But surely you will not affirm that the universe bears such a resemblance to a house that we can with the same certainty infer a similar cause, or that the analogy is here entire and perfect. The dissimilitude is so striking that the utmost you can here pretend to is a guess. . . .

"But allowing that we were to take the operations of one part of nature upon another for the foundation of our judgment concerning the origin of the whole (which never can be admitted), yet why select so minute, so weak, so bounded a principle as the reason and design of animals is found to be upon this planet? What peculiar privilege has this little agitation of the brain which we call thought, that we must thus make it the model of the whole universe? Our partiality in our own favor does indeed present it on all occasions, but sound philosophy ought carefully to guard against so natural an illusion. . . .

"And can you blame me, Cleanthes, if I here imitate the prudent reserve of Simonides, who, according to the noted story, being asked by Hiero, *What God was*? desired a day to think of it, and then two days more; and after that manner continually prolonged the term, without ever bringing in his definition or description? Could you even blame me if I had answered, at first, that I did not know, and was sensible that this subject lay vastly beyond the reach of my faculties? You might cry out skeptic . . . as much as you pleased: but, having found in so many other subjects much more familiar the imperfections and even contradictions of human reason, I never should expect any success from its feeble conjectures in a subject so sublime and so remote from the sphere of our observation. . . ." (Part II)

DEMEA (Christian with emphasis on faith but also on logic):

" . . . In reality, Cleanthes, consider what it is you assert, when you represent the deity as similar to a human mind and understanding. . . . New opinions, new passions, new affections, new feelings arise, which continually diversify the . . . [human] mental scene, and produce in it the greatest variety, and most rapid succession imaginable.

How is this compatible, with that perfect immutability and simplicity, which all true theists ascribe to the deity?"

PHILO (skeptic):

[Also addressing Cleanthes: "And]...how... shall we satisfy ourselves concerning the cause of that Being whom you suppose the Author of nature, or, according to your system of anthropomorphism, the ideal world.... If the material world rests upon a similar ideal world, this ideal world must rest upon some other, and so on without end. It were better, therefore, never to look beyond the present material world.... (Part IV)

"And why not become a perfect anthropomorphite? Why not assert the deity or deities to be corporeal, and to have eyes, a nose, mouth, ears, etc.? Epicurus maintained that no man had ever seen reason but in a human figure; therefore, the gods must have a human figure. And this argument, which is deservedly so much ridiculed by Cicero, becomes, according to you, solid and philosophical.

"In a word, Cleanthes, a man who follows your hypothesis is able, perhaps, to assert or conjecture that the universe sometime arose from something like design; but beyond that position he cannot ascertain one single circumstance, and is left afterwards to fix every point of his theology by the utmost license of fancy and hypothesis. This world, for aught he knows, is very faulty and imperfect, compared to a superior standard, and was only the first rude essay of some infant deity who afterwards abandoned it, ashamed of his lame performance; it is the work only of some dependent, inferior deity, and is the object of derision to his superiors; it is the production of old age and dotage in some superannuated deity, and ever since his death has run on at adventures, from the first impulse and active force which it received from him. You justly give signs of horror, Demea, at these strange suppositions; but these, and a thousand more of the same kind, are Cleanthes's suppositions, not mine. From the moment the attributes of the Deity are supposed finite, all these have place. And I cannot, for my part, think that so wild and unsettled a system of theology is, in any respect, preferable to none at all. . . ." (Part V)

. . . Philo continued. . . . "A tree bestows order and organization on that tree which springs from it . . . ; an animal in the same manner on its offspring; a bird on its nest; and instances of this kind are even more frequent in the world than those of order which arise from reason and contrivance. . . . Why an orderly system may not be spun from the belly as well as from the brain, it will be difficult for . . . Cleanthes to give a satisfactory reason. . . . (Part VII)

["But let us set this abstract argument aside for a moment"] . . . , said Philo, ["and consider] the curious artifices of nature, . . . [that] embitter the life of every living being. The stronger prey upon the weaker, and keep them in perpetual terror and anxiety. The weaker too, in their turn, often prey upon the stronger. . . . On each hand, before and behind, above and below, every animal is surrounded with enemies, which incessantly seek his misery and destruction. . . .

"Man, it is true, can, by combination, surmount all his real enemies, and become master of the whole animal creation; but does he not immediately raise up to himself imaginary enemies, the demons of his fancy, who haunt him with superstitious terrors, and blast every enjoyment of life? His pleasure, as he imagines, becomes in their eyes a crime; his food and repose give them umbrage and offense; his very sleep and dreams furnish new materials to anxious fear; and even death, his refuge from every other ill, presents only the dread of endless and innumerable woes....

"Besides, . . . this very society, by which we surmount those wild beasts, our natural enemies, what new enemies does it not raise to us? What woe and misery does it not occasion? Man is the greatest enemy of man. Oppression, injustice, contempt, contumely, violence, sedition, war, calumny, treachery, fraud—by these they mutually torment each other, and they would soon dissolve that society which they had formed, were it not for the dread of still greater ills, which must attend their separation....

"Is it possible, Cleanthes," said Philo, "that after all these reflections, and infinitely more, which might be suggested, you can still persevere in your anthropomorphism, and assert the moral attributes of the Deity, his justice, benevolence, mercy, and rectitude, to be of the same nature with these virtues in human creatures? His power, we allow, is infinite; whatever he wills is executed; but neither man nor any other animal is happy; therefore, he does not will their happiness. His wisdom is infinite; He is never mistaken in choosing the means to any end; but the course of nature tends not to human or animal felicity; therefore it is not established for that purpose. Through the whole compass of human knowledge, there are no inferences more certain and infallible than these. In what respect, then, do his benevolence and mercy resemble the benevolence and mercy of men?

"Epicurus's old questions are yet unanswered. Is he willing to prevent evil, but not able? Then is he impotent. Is he able, but not willing? Then is he malevolent. Is he both able and willing? Whence then is evil? . . .

"This is not, by any means, what we expect from infinite power, infinite wisdom, and infinite goodness. Why is there any misery at all in the world? . . . (Part X) There may be four hypotheses . . . framed concerning the first causes of the universe: that they are endowed with perfect goodness; that they have perfect malice; that they are opposite, and have both goodness and malice; that they have neither goodness nor malice. Mixed phenomena can never prove the two former unmixed principles; and the uniformity and steadiness of general laws seem to oppose the third. The fourth, therefore, seems by far the most probable...." (Part XI)

DEMEA (Christian with emphasis on faith, but also on logic):

" ... If so many difficulties attend the argument *a posteriori*," said Demea, "had we not better adhere to that simple and sublime argument *a priori* which, by offering to us infallible demonstration, cuts off at once all doubt and difficulty? ... For how can an effect, which either is finite, or, for aught we know, may be so—how can such an effect, I say, prove an infinite cause? The unity, too, of the Divine Nature, it is very difficult, if not absolutely impossible, to deduce merely from contemplating the works of nature....

"The [*a priori*] argument ... which I would insist on, is ... [as follows]. Whatever exists must have a cause or reason of its existence; it being absolutely impossible for anything to produce itself, or be the cause of its own existence. In mounting up, therefore, from effects to causes, we must either go on in tracing an infinite succession, without any ultimate cause at all; or must at last have recourse to some ultimate cause, that is necessarily existent. Now, . . . the first supposition is absurd. . . . The question . . . still . . . [remains] why this particular succession of causes existed from eternity, and not any other succession, or no succession at all. . . . We must, therefore, have recourse to a necessarily existent Being, who carries the reason of his existence in himself, and who cannot be supposed not to exist, without an express contradiction. There is, consequently, such a Being; that is, there is a deity."

CLEANTHES (Christian reconciler of faith and reason, with emphasis on experience):

"I shall not leave it to Philo," said Cleanthes, "to point out the weakness of . . . [Demea's endorsement of a purely logical proof, unrelated to experience, for the existence of God]. It seems to me so obviously ill-grounded, and at the same time of so little consequence to the cause of true piety and religion, that I shall myself venture to show the fallacy of it.

"I shall begin with observing, that there is an evident absurdity in pretending to demonstrate a matter of fact, or to prove it by any arguments *a priori*. Nothing is demonstrable unless the contrary implies a contradiction.... [But]... whatever we conceive as existent, we can also conceive as non-existent. There is no being, therefore, whose non-existence implies a contradiction. Consequently there is no being, whose existence is demonstrable. I propose this argument as entirely decisive, and am willing to rest the whole controversy upon it.

"It is pretended that the Deity is a necessarily existent being; and this necessity of his existence is attempted to be explained by asserting, that if we knew his whole essence or nature, we should perceive it to be as impossible for him not to exist, as for twice two not to be four. But it is evident that this can never happen, while our faculties remain the same as at present. It will still be possible for us, at any time, to conceive the non-existence of what we formerly conceived to exist.... The words, therefore, necessary existence, have no meaning; or, which is the same thing; none that is consistent...."

PHILO (skeptic):

"Though the reasonings which you have urged, Cleanthes, may well excuse me," said Philo, "from starting any further difficulties, yet I cannot forbear insisting still upon another ... [argument]. It is observed by arithmeticians, that the products of 9, compose always either 9, or some ... product of 9, if you add together all the characters of which any of the former products is composed. Thus, of 18, 27, 36, which are products of 9, you make 9 by adding 1 to 8, 2 to 7, 3 to 6. Thus, 369 is a product also of 9; and if you add 3, 6, and 9, you make 18, a ... product of 9. To a superficial observer, so wonderful a regularity may be admired as the effect either of chance or design; but a skillful algebraist immediately concludes it to be the work of necessity, and demonstrates that it must forever result from the nature of these numbers. Is it not probable, I ask, that the whole economy of the universe is conducted by a like necessity, though no human algebra can furnish a key which solves the difficulty? And instead of admiring the order of natural beings, may it not happen, that, could we penetrate into the intimate nature of bodies, we should clearly see why it was absolutely impossible they could ever admit of any other disposition? So dangerous is it to introduce this idea of necessity into the present question! And so naturally does it afford an inference directly opposite to the religious hypothesis! . . . (Part IX)

"[But there is only so far we can go in this way.] . . . All men of sound reason are disgusted with verbal disputes, which abound so much in philosophical and theological inquiries; and it is found, that the only remedy for this abuse must arise from clear definitions, from the precision of those ideas which enter into any argument, and from the strict and uniform use of those terms which are employed. But there is a species of controversy, which, from the very nature of language and of human ideas, is involved in perpetual ambiguity, and can never, by any precaution or any definitions, be able to reach a reasonable certainty or precision. These are the controversies concerning the degrees of any quality or circumstance. Men may argue to all eternity, whether Hannibal be a great, or a very great, or a superlatively great man, what degree of beauty Cleopatra possessed. . . . That the dispute concerning theism is of this nature, and consequently is merely verbal, or perhaps, if possible, still more incurably ambiguous, will appear upon the slightest inquiry. . . .

" . . . This is well understood in the world; and none but fools ever repose less trust in a man, because they hear that from study and philosophy, he has entertained some speculative doubts with regard to theological subjects. And when we have to do with a man, who makes a great profession of religion and devotion, has this any other effect upon several, who pass for prudent, than to put them on their guard, lest they be cheated and deceived by him? . . .

" . . . It is contrary to common sense to entertain apprehensions or terrors upon account of any opinion whatsoever, or to imagine that we run any risk hereafter, by the freest use of our reason. Such a sentiment implies both an absurdity and an inconsistency. It is an absurdity to believe that the Deity has human passions, and one of the lowest of human passions, a restless appetite for applause. It is an inconsistency to believe, that, since the Deity has this human passion, he has not others also, and, in particular, a disregard to the opinions of creatures so much inferior." (Part XII)

Part Two: Morals

Although Hume was a determined enemy of religion in any form, and especially Christianity, he recognized that this left a gap in morals. If God or revealed religion was not to be the source of our morals, what was to take its place?

Could logic take its place? Could clear reasoning from a self-evident (*a priori*) premise to conclusion and then to corollary of the conclusion and then onward from there show us the right way to think about our lives and social relations with other human beings? Hume thought not.

Logic had its place, but only as a tool to help us order the practical lessons taught us by experience. We learn from experience what is both useful and agreeable, and no moral system makes sense if not useful and agreeable. Moreover experience teaches us that what is useful and agreeable in the long run is often of much greater consequence than what seems useful or agreeable at the moment, which is a supreme lesson.

All of this is of the greatest importance, but Hume adds a critical caveat. Even experience has a limited application. Only emotion, which Hume called sentiment, could prompt us to want to act on the wisdom to be gained from experience. We must want to be wise; indeed we must want to be happy. Not everyone actually makes this choice. Ultimately, therefore, morals are based on emotion.

This last point has led to great misunderstanding, as we shall shortly see. Hume does not mean that morals are all about emotion. He does not mean that they do not also include reason and experience as essential pillars. He certainly does not mean that our moral choices are without empirical or logical content, more like the barking of dogs than the considered judgments of human beings. He simply means that emotion gives us the energy and will to make the choices we make, and it is well for us to draw as much wisdom as we can from experience and even logic in making those choices.

It is, however, best to let Hume speak for himself in these matters. Here are a few thoughts of this remarkably kind, gentle, and humane enemy of religion on the proper way to go about developing our morals:

1. . . . A considerable part of [philosophy] . . . arise[s] either from the fruitless efforts of human vanity, which would penetrate into subjects utterly inaccessible to the understanding, or from the craft of popular superstitions which, being unable to defend themselves on fair ground, raise these entangling brambles to cover and protect their weakness. . . . (*An Enquiry Concerning Human Understanding*, Section I, 6)

2. . . . It seems to me, that the only objects [provable beyond doubt] . . . are quantity and number. . . .

All other enquiries of men regard only matter of fact and existence; and these are evidently incapable of . . . [absolute proof]. . . .

[Experience] . . . is the foundation of moral reasoning. . . .

[But] morals . . . are not so properly objects of the understanding as of taste and sentiment. Beauty, whether moral or natural, is felt, more properly than perceived. . . .

When we run over libraries, persuaded of these principles, what havoc must we make? If we take in our hand any volume; of divinity or school metaphysics, for instance; let us ask, *Does it contain any abstract reasoning concerning quantity or number?* No. *Does it contain any experimental reasoning concerning matter of fact and existence?* No. Commit it then to the flames: for it can contain nothing but sophistry and illusion. (Ibid., Section XII, Part III)

3. If we can depend upon any principle which we learn from philosophy, this, I think, may be considered as certain and undoubted, that there is nothing, in itself, valuable or despicable, desirable or hateful, beautiful or deformed; but that these attributes arise from the particular constitution and fabric of human sentiment and affection. . . . ("The Skeptic")

4. Some men are possessed of great strength of mind; and even when they pursue *external* objects, are not much affected by a disappointment, but renew their application and industry with the greatest cheerfulness. Nothing contributes more to happiness than such a turn of mind.

. . . The happiest disposition of mind is the *virtuous*; or, in other words, that which leads to action and employment, renders us sensible to the social passions, steels the heart against the assaults of fortune, reduces the affections to a just moderation, makes our own thoughts an entertainment to us, and inclines us rather to the pleasures of society and conversation than to those of the senses. . . .

Habit is another powerful means of reforming the mind, and implanting in it good dispositions and inclinations. . . .

. . . Though virtue be undoubtedly the best choice, when it is attainable, yet such is the disorder and confusion of man's affairs, that no perfect or regular distribution of happiness and misery is ever in this life to be expected. . . . (Ibid.)

5. None of . . . [us] can go beyond experience, or establish any principles which are not founded on that authority. Moral philosophy has, indeed, this peculiar disadvantage, which is not found in natural, that in collecting its experiments, it cannot make them purposely, with premeditation, and after such a manner as to satisfy itself concerning every particular difficulty which may arise. . . . We must therefore glean up our experiments in this science from a cautious observation of human life, and take them as they appear in the common course of the world, by men's behavior in company, in affairs, and in their pleasures. . . . (*A Treatise of Human Nature*, Introduction)

6. Morality consists not in any [logical] relations . . . ; but if examined, will prove with
equal certainty, that it consists not in any
matter of [indisputable] fact, which can
be discovered by the understanding. . . .

When you pronounce any action or character to be vicious, you mean nothing, but
that from the constitution of your nature
you have a feeling or sentiment of blame
from the contemplation of it. . . .

I cannot forbear adding to these reasonings an observation, which may, perhaps, be
found of some importance. In every system
of morality, which I have hitherto met with,
I have always remarked, that the author proceeds for some time in the ordinary way of
reasoning . . . , [making] observations concerning human affairs; when of a sudden I
am surprised to find, that instead of the usual
copulations of propositions, is, and is not,
I meet with no proposition that is not connected with an ought, or an ought not. This
change is imperceptible; but is, however, of
the last consequence. For as this ought, or
ought not, expresses some new relation or
affirmation, it is necessary that it should be
observed and explained; and at the same time

that a reason should be given, for what seems
altogether inconceivable, how this new relation can be a deduction from others, which
are entirely different from it. But as authors
do not commonly use this precaution, I shall
presume to recommend it to the readers;
and am persuaded, that this small attention
would subvert all the vulgar systems of morality, and let us see, that the distinction of
vice and virtue is not founded merely on
the relations of objects, nor is perceived by
reason. (Ibid., Book III, Part I, Section I)

Note: We have already observed that the preceding
argument, often summarized as "no ought from an is,"
may easily be misinterpreted. It does not mean there
is no relationship between the facts we think we glean
from observation or personal experience and our value
judgments. The latter are not just a witless expression
of emotion; Hume makes it clear that he draws conclusions from his personal experience that heavily influence his moral judgments. In his *An Enquiry Concerning the Principles of Morals*, Section I, published
only three years after *An Enquiry Concerning Human
Understanding*, he also states that mankind should
"reject every system of ethics, however subtle or ingenious, which is not founded on fact and observation."

So what then does Hume mean when he says we
should be careful about drawing an ought from an is,

a value judgment from what we believe to be a fact, based on observation and experience? In the first place, we are being warned that what we learn from experience depends on individual circumstances. It will not be exactly the same for everybody, even people of the same age. In the second place, the results of our actions are never "pure and unmixed." ("Of the Rise and Progress in the Arts and Sciences") In the third place, even if circumstances and outcomes were not so variable, knowledge gained from observation and experience would never give us absolutely certain knowledge, only probabilities.

Importantly, we also have to want to learn from the "facts" of experience, and want to make our lives better by doing so, or experience will be of no use to us. This desire to improve our lives does not itself come from either logic or experience. It must come from some other source within ourselves. It may be characterized as almost instinctive, built into us, but many people choose to act self-destructively, so it is clearly also a choice.

Can such imperfect knowledge gained from observation and experience, and put to use by our will, actually help us? Hume says yes. Moreover, he argues that such imperfect knowledge is much more valuable than what he characterizes as the spurious and misleading knowledge provided by religion and other systems not based on observation and experience. Hume's further comments will help clarify all this.

... The common rule [of government in civil society] requires submission; and it is only in cases of grievous tyranny and oppression, that the exception can take place. . . . (Ibid., Section X)

8. ... We shall endeavor to follow a very simple method . . . in collecting and arranging the estimable or blameable qualities of men. . . . We shall begin our enquiry on this head by the consideration of the social virtues, Benevolence and Justice. . . . (*An Enquiry Concerning the Principles of Morals*, Section I)

... May it not . . . [be] concluded, that the utility, resulting from the social virtues, forms, at least, a *part* of their merit, and is one source of that approbation and regard so universally paid to them? . . .

In [this instance and in] general, what praise is implied in the simple epithet *useful*! What reproach in the contrary!

In all determinations of morality, this circumstance of public utility is ever principally in view; and wherever disputes arise, either in philosophy or common life, concerning the bounds of duty, the question cannot, by any means, be decided with greater certainty, than by ascertaining, on any side, the true interests of mankind. . . .

[Experience teaches what is useful, which may take time and thought.] . . . Giving alms to common beggars is naturally praised; because it seems to carry relief to the distressed and indigent; but when we observe the encouragement thence arising to idleness and debauchery, we regard that species of charity rather as a weakness than a virtue. . . . that the homely bread of the honest and industrious is often thereby converted into delicious cakes for the idle and the prodigal, we soon retract our heedless praises. . . . (Ibid., Section II, Part II)

Note: Hume's view on alms to street beggars and public welfare continues to be disputed, which illustrates his principal that knowledge derived from observation and experience will always be imperfect and uncertain.

. . . It seems so natural a thought to ascribe to their utility the praise, which we bestow on the social virtues, that one would expect to meet with this principle everywhere in moral writers, as the chief foundation of their reasoning and enquiry. In common life, we may observe, that the circumstance of utility is always appealed to; nor is it supposed, that a greater eulogy can be given to any man, than to display his usefulness to the public, and enumerate the services, which he has performed to mankind and society. . . . (Ibid., Section V, Part I) What need we seek for abstruse and remote systems, when there occurs one so obvious and natural? . . . (Ibid., Section V, Part II)

[Beside the social virtues, there are many others such as] . . . *discretion, caution, enterprise, industry, assiduity, frugality, economy, good-sense, prudence, discernment, . . . temperance, sobriety, patience, constancy, perseverance, forethought, considerateness, . . . order, . . . presence of mind, quickness of conception, . . . [and] facility of expression . . .* which tend only to the utility of their possessor, without any reference to us, or to the community, [but yet] are esteemed and valued. . . . (Ibid., Section VI)

. . . Cheerfulness carries great merit with it, and naturally conciliates the goodwill of mankind. No quality, indeed, more readily communicates itself to all around; because no one has a greater propensity to display itself, in jovial talk and pleasant entertainment. The flame spreads through the whole circle; and the most sullen and morose are often caught by it. . . .

From this influence of cheerfulness, both to communicate itself and to engage approbation, we may perceive that there is another set of mental qualities, which, without any utility or any tendency to farther good, either of the community or of the possessor, diffuse a satisfaction on the beholders, and procure friendship and regard. Their immediate sensation, to the person possessed of them, is agreeable. . . .

In all polite nations and ages, a relish for pleasure, if accompanied with temperance and decency, is esteemed a considerable merit, even in the greatest men; and becomes still more requisite in those of inferior rank and character. . . . (Ibid., Section VII)

It may justly appear surprising that any man in so late an age, should find it requisite to prove, by elaborate reasoning, that Personal Merit consists altogether in the possession of mental qualities, *useful* or *agreeable* to the *person himself* or to *others*. . . . And as every quality which is useful or agreeable to ourselves or others is, in common life, allowed to be a part of personal merit; so no other will ever be received, where men judge of things by their natural, unprejudiced reason, without the delusive glosses of superstition and false religion.

It seems a happiness in the present theory, that it enters not into that vulgar dispute concerning the *degrees* of benevolence or self-love, which prevail in human nature. . . . It is sufficient for our present purpose, if it be allowed, what surely, without the greatest absurdity cannot be disputed, that there is some benevolence, however small, infused into our bosom; some spark of friendship for humankind; some particle of the dove kneaded into our frame, along with the elements of the wolf and serpent. . . .

What wonder then, that moral sentiments are found of such influence in life; though springing from principles, which may appear, at first sight, somewhat small and delicate? But these principles, we must remark, are social and universal; they form, in a manner, the *party* of humankind against vice or disorder, its common enemy.... Other passions, though perhaps originally stronger, yet being selfish and private, are often overpowered by its force, and yield the dominion of our breast to those social and public principles. ...

It must ... be allowed that every quality of the mind, which is *useful* or *agreeable* to the *person himself* or to *others*, communicates a pleasure to the spectator, engages his esteem, and is admitted under the honorable denomination of virtue or merit. ... Who can dispute that a mind, which supports a perpetual serenity and cheerfulness, a noble dignity and undaunted spirit, a tender affection and goodwill to all around; as it has more enjoyment within itself, is also a more animating and rejoicing spectacle, than if dejected with melancholy, tormented with anxiety, irritated with rage, or sunk into the most abject baseness and degeneracy? And as to the qualities, immediately *agreeable* to *others*, they speak sufficiently for themselves; and he must be unhappy, indeed, either in his own temper, or in his situation and company, who has never perceived the charms of a facetious wit or flowing affability, of a

say, between these and the feverish, empty amusements of luxury and expense? These natural pleasures, indeed, are really without price; both because they are below all price in their attainment, and above it in their enjoyment. (Ibid., Section IX, Part II)

If the foregoing hypothesis be received, . . . we may . . . examine how far either *reason* or *sentiment* enters into all decisions of praise or censure.

One principal foundation of moral praise being supposed to lie in the usefulness of any quality or action, it is evident that *reason* must enter for a considerable share in all decisions of this kind; since nothing but that faculty can instruct us in the tendency of qualities and actions, and point out their beneficial consequences to society and to their possessor. In many cases this is an affair liable to great controversy: doubts may arise; opposite interests may occur; and a preference must be given to one side, from very nice views, and a small overbalance of utility. . . .

But though reason, when fully assisted and improved, be sufficient to instruct us in the pernicious or useful tendency of qualities and actions; it is not alone sufficient to produce any moral blame or approbation. Utility is only a [means] to a certain end; and were the end totally indifferent to us, we should feel the same indifference towards the means. It is requisite a *sentiment* should here display itself, in order to give a preference to the useful above the pernicious tendencies. This *sentiment* can be no other than a feeling for the happiness of [myself and] mankind, and a resentment of their misery; since these are the different ends which virtue and vice have a tendency to promote. Here therefore *reason* instructs us in the several tendencies of actions, and *humanity* makes a distinction in favor of those which are useful and … [agreeable]. … (Ibid., Appendix I)

Note: Christians of Hume's day found his work scandalous for many reasons. First, they regarded religion as the only available bulwark against the human propensity for gluttony, sexual misconduct, anarchy, and violence, while Hume argued just the opposite, that virtue provided its own reward and religion just contributed to superstitious fears, fanaticism, and vice. The notion that chastity was a good idea because it was socially useful, not because sexual license was inherently sinful, even for women, was particularly shocking. The publisher of two of Hume's essays, "On Suicide" and "On the Immortality of the Soul," both withheld from publication during the author's lifetime, felt constrained in 1783 to protect himself from possible prosecution by denouncing his own publication in a preface. The intent of publication, the preface stated, was "to expose the . . . pitiful . . . sophistry of the author" and thus reveal "truth's superiority to error."

Not all of the fire directed at Hume came from the pulpit or popular press. Immanuel Kant, often considered the most important Western philosopher, said that he had been awakened from his "metaphysical slumbers" by Hume and set out to refute the idea that logic cannot give us reliable morals or that experience must be our only guide, however imperfect experience may be. Kant's defense of logic and rejection of experience as our moral guide are reviewed in Chapter Eleven.

Part Three: Economics

What David Hume Has to Teach Us Today

Reading David Hume on economics, one has the feeling that he is rebutting today's dominant Keynesian policies, the policies espoused by almost all world governments of our era. But how can this be, since Hume died in 1776 and Keynes in 1946? The explanation is simple: Keynesianism is not really new. It is in large part a revival of the old mercantilist ideas that Hume was vigorously attacking.

Keynes acknowledges at the end of his magnum opus, *The General Theory of Employment, Interest, and Money*, that he is reviving mercantilism. This is a bit unexpected by the reader, because earlier in the same book he states that he is staking out new ground in economics, but perhaps he means he is staking out new ground by reviving and updating mercantilism. Whatever the explanation, much of Hume seems highly relevant to current debates for and against Keynes, a proponent of government deficit spending to stimulate a weak economy and of government control of the money supply in order to bring down interest rates. On trade issues, Keynes took different positions at different times. He began as a Humean free trader, then became a protectionist, then returned to a generally free trade position after World War II.

Here is a little of what Hume actually said about eonomics:

1. We need better economic thinking.

Mankind are, in all ages, caught by the same baits: the same tricks played over and over again, still trepan them. ("Of Public Credit")

... It must be owned, that nothing can be of more use than to improve, by practice, the method of reasoning on these subjects,

which of all others are the most important, though they are commonly treated
in the loosest and most careless manner.
("Of Interest")

2. It is not money that makes a society rich.

Since wealth is measured in money, it is easy to con-
fuse the two. But it is the ability to produce that makes
us rich. If we add to the money supply without increasing the ability to produce, the result will just be higher
prices. As Hume explains:

> We fancy, because an individual would be
> much richer, were his stock of money dou-
> bled, that the same good effect would follow,
> were the money of every one increased; not
> considering that this would raise as much
> the price of every commodity, and reduce
> every man in time to the same condition
> as before. . . . ("Of the Balance of Trade")

> The prices of everything depend on the pro-
> portion between commodities and money,
> and . . . any considerable alteration on ei-
> ther has the same effect, either of heighten-
> ing or lowering the price. Increase the com-
> modities, they become cheaper; increase the
> money, they rise in their value.

It is also evident, that the prices do not so much depend on the absolute quantity of commodities and that of money, which are in a nation, as on that of the commodities, which come or may come to market, and of the money which circulates. If the coin be locked up in chests, it is the same thing with regard to prices, as if it were annihilated; if the commodities be hoarded in magazines and granaries, a like effect follows. As the money and commodities, in these cases, never meet, they cannot affect each other.

The necessary effect is, that, provided the money increase not in the nation, everything must become much cheaper in times of industry and refinement, than in rude, uncultivated ages.... ("Of Money")

Hume makes it clear that falling prices are a dividend of industry and should not be feared. Nor is it necessary for authorities to keep creating new money as an economy grows:

Here then we may learn the fallacy of the remark, often to be met with in historians, and even in common conversation, that any particular state is weak, though fertile, populous, and well cultivated, merely because it wants money. It appears, that the want of

> money can never injure any state within it-
> self: For men and commodities are the real
> strength of any community. ("Of Money")

Hume did, however, add a caveat to the idea that money is "neutral," that what matters is not the amount of money in circulation but rather a society's ability to produce. He noted that new money does not tend to fall into everyone's hands at once or evenly. New money often falls into the hands of a few people who have first use of it—before it has flowed into the economy and raised prices. Anyone with access to new money before it has altered economic calculations clearly has an advantage, because these fortunate people can use the new money to buy at pre-inflation prices. Because the process of injecting new money into an economy is not "neutral," it is unfair to most people:

> Though the high price of commodities be
> a necessary consequence of the increase of
> gold and silver, yet it follows not immedi-
> ately upon that increase; but some time is re-
> quired before the money circulates through
> the whole state, and makes its effect be felt
> on all ranks of people. At first, no alteration
> is perceived; by degrees the price rises, first
> of one commodity, then of another till the
> whole at last reaches a just proportion with
> the new quantity of specie which is in the

kingdom. In my opinion, it is only in this interval or intermediate situation, between the acquisition of money and rise of prices, that the increasing quantity of gold and silver is favorable to industry. When any quantity of money is imported into a nation, it is not at first dispersed into many hands, but is confined to the coffers of a few persons, who immediately seek to employ it to advantage. ("Of Money").

3. *Interest rates are affected by the quantity of money in an economy, but ultimately reflect other factors as well.*

Prices have risen near four times since the discovery of the Indies; and it is probable gold and silver have multiplied much more: but interest has not fallen much above half. The rate of interest, therefore, is not derived [solely] . . . from the quantity of the precious metals. . . .

High interest arises from *three* circumstances: a great demand for borrowing, little riches to supply that demand, and great profits arising from commerce: and the circumstances are a clear proof of the small advance of commerce and industry, not of the scarcity of gold and silver. Low interest, on the other hand, proceeds from the three opposite circumstances: a small demand for borrowing; great riches to supply that demand; and small profits arising from commerce....

... Suppose that, by miracle, every man in Great Britain should have five pounds slipped into his pocket in one night; this would much more than double the whole money that is at present in the kingdom; yet there would not next day, nor for some time, be any more lenders, nor any variation in the interest. And were there nothing but landlords and peasants in the state, this money, however abundant, could never gather into sums, and would only serve to increase the prices of everything, without any further consequence....

A ... reason of ... [the] popular mistake with regard to the cause of low interest, seems to be the instance of some nations, where, after a sudden acquisition of money, or of the precious metals by means of foreign conquest, the interest has fallen not only among them, but in all the neighboring states, as soon as that money was dispersed, and had insinuated itself into every corner. Thus, interest in Spain fell near a half immediately after the discovery of the West Indies, as we are informed by Garcilasso de la Vega; and it has been ever since gradually sinking in every kingdom of Europe. . . .

In the conquering country, it is natural to imagine that this new acquisition of money will fall into a few hands, and be gathered into large sums, which seek a secure revenue, either by the purchase of land or by interest; and consequently the same effect follows, for a little time, as if there had been a great accession of industry and commerce. The increase of lenders above the borrowers sinks the interest, and so much the faster if those who have acquired those large sums find no industry or commerce in the state, and no method of employing their money but by lending it at interest.

But after this new mass of gold and silver has been digested, and has circulated through the whole state, affairs will soon return to their former situation, while the landlords and new money-holders, living idly, squander above their income; and the former daily contract debt, and the latter encroach on their stock till its final extinction. The whole money may

> still be in the state, and make itself felt by the
> increase of prices; but not being now collected
> into any large masses or stocks, the dispro-
> portion between the borrowers and lenders
> is the same as formerly, and consequently
> the high interest returns.... ("Of Interest")

Hume goes on to explain that interest can only be
lowered over the long run, not by financial manipu-
lations, but by increasing production. As production
increases, producer profits will also fall:

> ... It must be owned, that nothing can be
> of more use than to improve, by practice,
> the method of reasoning on these subjects,
> which of all others are the most important,
> though they are commonly treated in the
> loosest and most careless manner.

> An increase of commerce, by a necessary
> consequence, raises a great number of lend-
> ers, and by that means produces lowness of
> interest. We must now consider how far this
> increase of commerce diminishes the prof-
> its arising from that profession, and gives
> rise to the *third* circumstance requisite to
> produce lowness of interest....

> When commerce has become extensive, and
> employs large stocks, there must arise rivalries

among the merchants, which diminish the profits of trade, at the same time that they increase the trade itself. The low profits of merchandise induce the merchants to accept more willingly of a low interest when they leave off business, and begin to indulge themselves in ease and indolence. It is needless, therefore, to inquire, which of these circumstances, to wit, *low interest* or *low profits*, is the cause, and which the effect? They both arise from an extensive commerce, and mutually forward each other. . . .

No man will accept of low profits where he can have high interest; and no man will accept of low interest where he can have high profits. An extensive commerce, by producing large stocks, diminishes both interest and profits, and is always assisted, in its diminution of the one, by the proportional sinking of the other. I may add, that, as low profits arise from the increase of commerce and industry, they serve in their turn to its further increase, by rendering the commodities cheaper, encouraging the consumption, and heightening the industry. And thus, if we consider the whole connection of causes and effects, interest is the barometer of the state, and

its lowness is a sign, almost infallible, of
the flourishing condition of a people. . . .
("Of Interest")

4. **Paper money, whether issued by governments
or banks, is injurious to an economy, because
it leads to price inflation. The practice
whereby banks are allowed to create the
equivalent of paper money by lending money
they do not possess (fractional reserve
banking) should be abolished.**

> Institutions of banks, funds, and paper credit,
> with which we in the Kingdom are so much
> infatuated, . . . render paper equivalent to
> money, circulate it through the whole state,
> make it supply the place of gold and silver,
> raise proportionately the price of labor and
> commodities, and by that means . . . ban-
> ish a great part of those precious metals. . . .
> What can be more shortsighted than our
> reasoning on this head . . . [since the pro-
> duction of this faux money just] raise[s] the
> price of every commodity.
>
> It must be allowed that no bank would be
> more advantageous, than such alone as . . .
> never augmented the circulating coin. ("Of
> Money")

Hume even pointed to the Bank of Amsterdam that was run on these 100% reserve lines. It kept custody of funds and lent money out as agent for the owner, but never lent money it did not possess, and therefore did not create new money as banks continue to do to this day.

5. Commodities are worth what someone will pay for them, not what they cost to produce.

Hume's friend Adam Smith claimed the opposite in his *The Wealth of Nations*. This error was in turn reproduced in Karl Marx's labor theory of value, where it had an immense impact on Communist doctrine and therefore on world history. Hume caught the error when, close to dying, he received an early copy of *The Wealth of Nations*. It took other economists another century to realize that Hume was right and Smith wrong. By then Marx's Communism was already a well-established ideology.

Smith, in earlier years, had been something of a protégé of Hume's, and held views closer to his mentor's. Smith's embrace of fractional reserve banking in *The Wealth of Nations*, contrary to Hume's teaching, also had an immense impact on subsequent world history, because the resulting fragility of the banking system greatly contributed to cycles of boom and bust that plagued the global market system.

6. Foreign trade does not mean "Beggar Thy Neighbor."

Hume forcefully argued that international trade is not a ruthless competition, a zero-sum game in which the gains of one nation can only come at the expense of another. It should least of all be seen as an extension of war by other means, and should not even be considered "an affair of state." ("Of Civil Liberty") On the contrary, trade is advantageous for both parties; both parties should equally be winners:

> Nothing is more usual, among states which have made some advances in commerce, than to look on the progress of their neighbors with a suspicious eye, to consider all trading states as their rivals, and to suppose that it is impossible for any of them to flourish, but at their expense. In opposition to this narrow and malignant opinion, I will venture to assert, that the increase of riches and commerce in any one nation, instead of hurting, commonly promotes the riches and commerce of all its neighbors; and that a state can scarcely carry its trade and industry very far, where all the surrounding states are buried in ignorance, sloth, and barbarism. . . .

> I shall therefore venture to acknowledge, that, not only as a man, but as a British subject, I pray for the flourishing commerce of Germany, Spain, Italy, and even France itself. I am at least certain, that Great Britain, and all those nations, would flourish more, did their sovereigns and ministers adopt such enlarged and benevolent sentiments towards each other.... ("Of the Balance of Trade")

Hume also exploded the idea that the purpose of trade was to attract money from trade rivals, which could then be hoarded:

> These errors, one may say, are gross and palpable; but there still prevails, even in nations well acquainted with commerce, a strong jealousy with regard to the balance of trade, and a fear that all their gold and silver may be leaving them. This seems to me, almost in every case, a groundless apprehension; and I should as soon dread, that all our springs and rivers should be exhausted, as that money should abandon a kingdom where there are people and industry....

> Suppose four-fifths of all the money in Great Britain to be annihilated in one night, and the nation reduced to the same condition, with regard to specie, as in the reigns

7. The pursuit of wealth is not an evil, but generally good for a society, especially when compared to the alternatives.

This point is not part of economics per se, but Hume's sociological argument is worth noting:

> There is no craving or demand of the human mind more constant and insatiable than that for exercise and employment; and this desire seems the foundation of most of our passions and pursuits. Deprive a man of all business and serious occupation, he runs restless from one amusement to another; and the weight and oppression which he feels from idleness is so great, that he forgets the ruin which must follow him from his immoderate expenses. Give him a more harmless way of employing his mind or body, he is satisfied, and feels no longer that insatiable thirst after pleasure. But if the employment you give him be lucrative, especially if the profit be attached to every particular exertion of industry, he has gain so often in his eye, that he acquires, by degrees, a passion for it, and knows no such pleasure as that of seeing the daily increase of his fortune. And this is the reason why trade increases frugality, and why, among merchants, there

is the same over-plus of misers above prodigals, as among the possessors of land there
is the contrary. ("Of Interest")

Hume also expressed admiration for merchants, whose
occupation was looked down upon at that time in Britain:

Merchants [are] . . . one of the most useful
races of men, who serve as agents between
those parts of the state that are wholly un-
acquainted, and are ignorant of each other's necessities. . . . ("Of Interest")

8. Government borrowing that is never repaid is an evil.

Government borrowing and borrowing anew to repay
old debts, which are thus never really paid off, was a new
idea in Hume's day. He thought it would end badly:

. . . Our modern expedient, which has become very general, is to mortgage the public
revenues, and to trust that posterity will pay
off the encumbrances contracted by their an-
cestors: and they, having before their eyes so
good an example of their wise fathers, have
the same prudent reliance on *their* posterity; who, at last, from necessity more than
choice, are obliged to place the same confidence in a new posterity. . . . [This is] . . .

a practice which appears ruinous beyond all controversy. . . .

It is very tempting to a minister to employ such an expedient, as enables him to make a great figure during his administration, without overburdening the people with taxes, or exciting any immediate clamors against himself. The practice, therefore, of contracting debt, will almost infallibly be abused in every government. It would scarcely be more imprudent to give a prodigal son a credit in every banker's shop in London, than to empower a statesman to draw bills, in this manner, upon posterity.

What, then, shall we say to the new paradox, that public encumbrances are, of themselves, advantageous, independent of the necessity of contracting them. . . . Reasonings such as these might naturally have passed for trials of wit among [ancient] . . . rhetoricians, had we not seen such absurd maxims patronized by great ministers, and by a whole party among us. . . .

[We are told that] . . . public securities are with us become a kind of money, and pass as readily at the current price as gold or silver. . . . In short our national debts furnish merchants with a species of money that is continually multiplying in their hands, and produces sure gain, besides the profits of their commerce....

We have indeed been told, that the public is no weaker on account of its debts, since they are mostly due among ourselves, and bring as much property to one as they take from another. It is like transferring money from the right hand to the left, which leaves the person neither richer nor poorer than before. Such loose reasoning and specious comparisons will always pass where we judge not upon principles. I ask, "Is it possible, in the nature of things, to overburden a nation with taxes.... But if all our present taxes be mortgaged, must we not invent new ones? And may not this matter be carried to a length that is ruinous and destructive?" ...

It must, indeed, be one of these two events; either the nation must destroy public credit, or public credit will destroy the nation. It is impossible that they can both subsist....

It is not altogether improbable, that when the nation becomes heartily sick of their debts, and is cruelly oppressed by them, some daring projector may arise with visionary schemes for their discharge. And as public credit will begin, by that time, to be a little frail, the least touch will destroy it. . . .

Mankind are, in all ages, caught by the same baits: the same tricks played over and over again, still trepan them.

The heights of popularity and patriotism are still the beaten road to power and tyranny; flattery, to treachery; standing armies to arbitrary government; and the glory of God to the temporal interest of the clergy. ("Of Public Credit")

The source of degeneracy which may be remarked in free governments, consists in the practice of contracting debt, and mortgaging the public revenues, by which taxes may, in time, become altogether intolerable. . . . The practice is of modern date. ("Of Civil Liberty")

9. *Slavery is an evil, whether regarded morally or from the point of view of economics.*

Hume was among the crusaders against the slavery of his time:

The remains which are found of domestic slavery, in the American colonies, and among some European nations, would never surely create a desire of rendering it more universal. The little humanity commonly observed in persons accustomed, from their infancy, to exercise so great authority over their fellow-creatures, and to trample upon human nature, were sufficient alone to disgust us with that unbounded dominion....

... Slavery is in general disadvantageous both to the happiness and populousness of mankind, and ... its place is much better supplied by the practice of hired servants.... ("Of the Populousness of Ancient Nations")

10. *Humanity needs government for order but government itself must be restrained by laws.*

Part Four: Political Philosophy

Hume is not currently much regarded as a political philosopher, although in his own day he was best known as the author of a multi-volume history of Britain which included many important political observations. There are also many political comments from his books and essays worth noting:

Reserve or disguise ... are always employed by those who enter upon any new project ...

in . . . government, or endeavor to inno-
vate. . . . ("Of the Protestant Succession")

We are . . . to look upon all the vast appara-
tus of our government, as having ultimately
no other object or purpose but the distribution of justice. . . .

All men are sensible of the necessity of justice to maintain peace and order; and all
men are sensible of the necessity of peace
and order for the maintenance of society. . . .
("Of the Origin of Government")

It is a question with several, whether there
be any essential difference between one form
of government and another and, whether
every form may not become good or bad,
according as it is well or ill administered? . . .
But here it may be proper to make a distinction. All absolute governments must very
much depend on the administration; and
this is one of the great inconveniences attending that form of government. Legislators, therefore, ought not to trust the future
government of a state entirely to chance, but
ought to provide a system of laws to regulate the administration of public affairs. . . .
Good laws may beget order and moderation
in the government, where the manners and

customs have instilled little humanity or justice into the tempers of men.... ("That Politics May be Reduced to a Science")

... It is impossible for the arts and sciences to arise, at first, among any people, unless that people enjoy the blessing of a free government. ("Of the Rise and Progress of the Arts and Sciences")

Chapter 10

Adam Smith
(1723–1790)

Why We All Need to Read Adam Smith

THERE ARE MANY myths about Adam Smith. Best-selling economist John Kenneth Galbraith claimed that Smith was "the first economist,"[104] and thus in effect the inventor of economics. This is certainly wrong. Smith was not even the inventor of modern free market economics. That accolade would be shared by Richard Cantillon,[105] Anne-Robert-Jacques Turgot,[106] David Hume,[107] and to a lesser degree François Quesnay,[108] among others.

Famed economist Joseph Schumpeter concluded rightly that "*The Wealth of Nations* does not contain a single analytic idea, principle, or method that was entirely new in 1776."[109] A journal article has even been devoted to the question of whether Smith was a plagiarist,[110] although the charge remains unproven, and probably applies today's standard to the past in an inappropriate way.

It is closer to the truth, but still incorrect, to say that *The Wealth of Nations* is the "bible" of free market capitalism. As we shall see, Smith made too many errors for this to be the case. A very prominent free market economist, Murray Rothbard, regarded Smith, in Rothbard colleague David Gordon's telling phrase, as almost the "gravedigger," not the founder of free market economics.[111]

If Rothbard were entirely right, we could stop right here, eliminate this chapter, and not bother to read Smith himself. To reach this conclusion, however, would be an error. There are reasons not only to read Smith, but also to study and value his work highly. In this chapter at least, we have come not to bury Smith for his undeniable faults but to praise him.

No one disputes that Smith is one of the most influential economists, and indeed thinkers, of world history. Economist Mark Skousen wrote a book describing the "big three" of economics as Smith, Marx, and Keynes. These three have clearly been the most influential, and

Smith the most lastingly influential of the three. Has any single book had a greater impact on world history than *The Wealth of Nations*? The only possible competitor is Charles Darwin's *Origin of the Species*, which ignited the evolution controversy.

Is then Smith, the uber-famous economist, simply overblown, a case of earning a reputation he does not deserve? No, not at all. Whatever his failings, he has more than earned his fame as the most profound and persuasive critic of an economic system traditionally referred to as mercantilism, but more recently (and quite appropriately) called "crony capitalism." Smith's critique is always relevant, because crony capitalism is the dominant economic system of world history. It is especially relevant today, when this type of capitalism is especially strong, both in the developed and the developing world.

What exactly is crony capitalism? In simple terms, we can think of it as state-led capitalism gone awry. In ideal terms, state-led capitalism envisions wise, unselfish, and far-sighted public servants making economic decisions for the greater good of all of us. In reality, critics of state-led capitalism say, public servants are rarely wise and far-sighted and never unselfish. They have their own interests, which in the case of politicians focus on the immediate need to get re-elected, with the true public welfare, and especially the true long-term public welfare, mostly ignored.

Public "servants" running the economy to serve their own interests are bad enough. But we get crony capitalism when the public servants reach out to ally themselves with rich people, corporations, labor unions, trial lawyers, or other powerful private interest groups. Often these alliances are formed under the fig leaf of government "regulating" the powerful private interests. But the reality is that government and special interests work out deals behind the regulatory smokescreen, in effect combine to run the economy for their mutual immediate advantage, not the long-term advantage of the general public, which government is sworn to serve.

Smith's solution to this conundrum is not to try to make regulation more honest or more effective. That, he suggests, is mostly futile. It is futile because government will never be honest enough to avoid the temptations of crony capitalism or wise enough to run the economy even if it could avoid the temptations. Indeed, no one can be wise enough to run the economy. Only the preferences of millions of consumers expressed through markets can successfully order and guide our economic affairs.

The correct solution is to get government out of the economy and make markets freer. Competition, encouraged by free markets, is, in the final analysis, the only reliable regulator of economic life. It is not surprising that powerful private economic interests hate competition and conspire with government regulators to restrict it and create government-supported monopolies.

One of the most egregious myths about Adam Smith is that he was an apologist for powerful private interests such as rich businessmen. In this account, Smith is often described as a "conservative" economist concerned with protecting the status quo. This is absurd. It ignores what Smith actually said.

Although certainly no firebrand, Smith was more of a "revolutionary" than a "conservative." His aim in writing *The Wealth of Nations* was to attack the status quo of his day, which was crony capitalist to its core. He wanted to get government out of the economy for many reasons, but especially because he thought the marriage of money and politics created an inherently corrupt system.

We can all talk endlessly about combating corruption and cleaning up the system. But, Smith infers, this will never happen under state-led capitalism. So long as government runs the economy, private economic interests will insinuate themselves into politics. Money and power will flow back and forth through ever more corrupted channels, the same channels which today run between The City and Whitehall in the UK, Wall Street and Washington in the US, among other murky streams. Average citizens always end up getting the short end of the stick, as they did during the infamous bailout of The City and Wall Street following the Crash of 2008, and during subsequent years of high unemployment.

Capitalism has been called by some a system run for the benefit of business owners. If so, this is not Smith's capitalism. He wants a system run for the benefit, not of the business owner or the worker, but of the average consumer. Of course, consumers are also workers; that is how they get the wherewithal to consume. But working, like organizing and owning businesses, is a means to an end: the creation of goods and services to meet the genuine needs of the people, and not just some of the people, all of the people, especially people still living in poverty.

Smith emphasizes that

> no society can surely be flourishing and happy,
> of which the far greater part of the members are poor and miserable.[112]

But in a crony capitalist system, not only the interests of the poor,

> [even] . . . the interest[s] of the [average]
> consumer [are] constantly sacrificed[113]

to those of rulers and special interests allied with the rulers.

Government ought to be impartial in its promotion of the common good:

> To hurt, in any degree, the interest of any
> one order of citizens, for no other reason

but to promote that of some other, is evidently contrary to that justice and equality of treatment which the sovereign owes to all the different orders of his subjects.[114]

Nevertheless,

it is the industry which is carried on for the benefit of the rich and the powerful, that is principally encouraged by our mercantile system. That which is carried on for the benefit of the poor and the indigent is too often either neglected or oppressed.[115]

Proponents of state-led capitalism often point to the selfishness and self-interested maneuvering of private business interests. Smith agrees with them up to a point:

The clamor and sophistry of merchants and manufacturers easily persuade them, that the private interest of a part, and of a subordinate part, of the society, is the general interest of the whole.

People of the same trade seldom meet together, even for merriment and diversion, but the conversation ends in a conspiracy against the public, or in some contrivance to raise prices.

The interest of the dealers . . . in any particular branch of trade or manufactures, is always in some respects different from, and even opposite to, that of the public. To widen the market, and to narrow the competition, is always the interest of the dealers. To widen the market may frequently be agreeable enough to the interest of the public; but to narrow the competition must always be against it, and can only serve to enable the dealers, by raising their profits above what they naturally would be, to levy, for their own benefit, an absurd tax upon the rest of their fellow citizens.

The proposal of any new law or regulation of commerce which comes from this order, ought always to be listened to with great precaution, and ought never to be adopted till after having been long and carefully examined, not only with the most scrupulous, but with the most suspicious attention. It comes from an order of men, whose interest is never exactly the same with that of the public, who have generally an interest to deceive and even to oppress the public, and who accordingly have, upon many occasions, both deceived and oppressed it.

Is state leadership and regulation possibly solving this perennial problem? No, says Smith. When private interests abuse power, they are merely doing what government itself does. And it is the takeover of government by private interests, under guise of being controlled by government, which is especially to be feared:

> The capricious ambition of kings and ministers has not, during the present and the preceding century, been more fatal to the repose of Europe, than the impertinent jealousy of merchants and manufacturers. The violence and injustice of the rulers of mankind is an ancient evil, for which, I am afraid, the nature of human affairs can scarce admit of a remedy. But the mean rapacity, the monopolizing spirit, of merchants and manufacturers, who neither are, nor ought to be, the rulers of mankind, though it cannot, perhaps, be corrected, may very easily be prevented from disturbing the tranquillity of anybody but themselves.

When government and private interest increasingly merge, we have what Smith called the "mercantile system," and much of *The Wealth of Nations* is spent describing its features. Among them are:

1. A Larger-than-Necessary Military Establishment

This appeals to the vainglory of public officials and offered many profit opportunities for well-connected private interests.

2. Colonies

Although overt colonialism has fallen out of fashion since the 18th century, imperialism has traditionally accompanied an overly large military, and afforded similar scope for vainglory or private profit.

3. Slavery

This was a notable feature of Smith's time, which he and similar-minded reformers vigorously opposed. Smith made the salient point that slavery was actually an uneconomic system that could only be maintained through government subsidy and enforcement:

> The work done by freemen comes cheaper in the end than that performed by slaves. It is found to be so even at Boston, New York, and Philadelphia, where the wages of common labor are so high.[116]

4. Government-Sponsored Monopoly

Everyone, governments included, pays lip service to the proposition that

> monopoly ... is a great enemy to good man-
> agement. .... [The best management] ...
> can never be universally established, but
> in consequence of that free and universal
> competition which forces everyone to have
> recourse to it for the sake of self-defense.[117]

Business owners know from experience that monopoly is difficult to fashion and impossible to sustain in a
truly free market. They, therefore, seek and very often
receive assistance from government in erecting trade
barriers. These barriers are never acknowledged for
what they are—they are justified as quality or safety
controls, when their real purpose is to restrict supply
and increase price. Smith offers many examples:

> [Government interferes with natural sup-
> ply and demand] in the three following
> ways. First, by restraining the competition
> in some employments to a smaller number
> than would otherwise be disposed to enter
> into them; secondly, by increasing it in oth-
> ers beyond what it naturally would be; and,
> thirdly, by obstructing the free circulation
> of labor and stock, both from employment
> to employment, and from place to place.

> In Sheffield, no master cutler can have more
> than one apprentice at a time, by a by-law of

the corporation. In Norfolk and Norwich, no master weaver can have more than two apprentices, under pain of forfeiting five pounds a month to the king. No master hatter can have more than two apprentices anywhere in England or in the English plantations, under pain of forfeiting; five pounds a month, half to the king, and half to him who shall sue in any court of record. Both these regulations . . . have been confirmed by a public law of the kingdom.

But the 5th of Elizabeth, commonly called the Statute of Apprenticeship, it was enacted that no person should, for the future, exercise any trade [or] craft at that time exercised in England, unless he had previously served to it an apprenticeship of seven years at least; and what before had been the by-law of many particular corporations, became in England the general and public law of all trades carried on in market towns.

These examples are particular to the 18th century and earlier. But government-sponsored monopoly is, if anything, more prevalent in today's economy. In the United States, for example, drugs are generally regarded as the most profitable major industry. And it is not hard to see why.

Each successful new drug is a government-sanctioned monopoly, guarded first by a government-granted patent and second by government approval from the Food and Drug Administration (FDA). Moreover, only government-approved drugs or equipment or procedures may be marketed as a treatment for any disease or health condition. If a food or supplement producer claims a health benefit, the government will quickly shut it down under penalty of fines or even jail.

To get a drug approved, it is common knowledge that company officials must have personal relationships with those inside the government, and it is therefore essential to hire former government employees at attractive salaries. Unfortunately, this is only one example of contemporary government-sponsored monopoly: they are virtually everywhere in modern economies, just as they were everywhere in Adam Smith's day.

5. Barriers to Free Trade

One of the many ways private interests, working with government, attempt to create monopolies is by erecting international trade barriers. They do this under the pretense of protecting domestic jobs, but this is just a subterfuge. As Smith notes:

> [It] cannot be doubted . . . that it was the
> spirit of monopoly which originally both
> invented and propagated this doctrine [of

trade protectionism] and they who first taught it were by no means such fools as they who believed it. In every country it always is, and must be, the interest of the great body of the people, to buy whatever they want of those who sell it cheapest. The proposition is so very manifest, that it seems ridiculous to take any pains to prove it; nor could it ever have been called in question, had not the interested sophistry of merchants and manufacturers confounded the common sense of mankind.

To give the monopoly of the home market to the produce of domestic industry, in any particular art or manufacture, is in some measure to direct private people in what manner they ought to employ their capitals, and must, in almost all cases, be either a useless or a hurtful regulation. If the produce of domestic [origin] can be brought there as cheap as that of foreign industry, the regulation is evidently useless. If it cannot, it must generally be hurtful.

It is the maxim of every prudent master of a family, never to attempt to make at home what it will cost him more to make than to buy. The tailor does not attempt to make his own shoes, but buys them off the shoemaker. The shoemaker does not attempt to make his own clothes, but employs a tailor. The farmer attempts to make neither the one nor the other, but employs those different artificers. All of them find it for their interest to employ their whole industry in a way in which they have some advantage over their neighbors, and to purchase with a part of its produce, or, what is the same thing, with the price of a part of it, whatever else they have occasion for.

What is prudence in the conduct of every private family can scarce be folly in that of a great kingdom. If a foreign country can supply us with a commodity cheaper than we ourselves can make it, better buy it of them with some part of the produce of our own industry, employed in a way in which we have some advantage.

The same maxim which would in this manner direct the common sense of one, or ten, or twenty individuals, should regulate the judgment of one, or ten, or twenty millions, and should make a whole nation regard the riches of its neighbors, as a probable cause and occasion for itself to acquire riches. A nation that would enrich itself by foreign trade is certainly most likely to do so, when its neighbors are all rich, industrious, and commercial nations. A great nation, surrounded on all sides by wandering savages and poor barbarians, might, no doubt, acquire riches by the cultivation of its own lands, and by its own interior commerce, but not by foreign trade.

Nothing . . . can be more absurd than [the] whole doctrine of the balance of trade, upon which, not only these restraints, but almost all the other regulations of commerce, are founded. When two places trade with one another, this doctrine supposes that, if the balance be even, neither of them either loses or gains; but if it leans in any degree to one side, that one of them loses, and the other gains, in proportion to its declension from the exact equilibrium. Both suppositions are false. A trade, which is forced by means of bounties and monopolies, may be, and commonly is, disadvantageous to the country in whose favor it is meant to be established, as I shall endeavor to show hereafter. But that trade which, without force or constraint, is naturally and regularly carried on between any two places, is always advantageous, though not always equally so, to both.

By advantage or gain, I understand, not the increase of the quantity of gold and silver [the money of Smith's day], but that of the exchangeable value of the annual produce of the land and labor of the country, or the increase of the annual revenue of its inhabitants.

There is another balance . . . which [is] . . . very different from the balance of trade, and which, according as it happens to be either favorable or unfavorable, necessarily occasions the prosperity or decay of every nation. This is the balance of the annual produce and consumption. If the exchangeable value of the annual produce, it has already been observed, exceeds that of the annual consumption, the capital of the society must annually increase in proportion to this excess. The society in this case lives within its revenue; and what is annually saved out of its revenue, is naturally added to its capital, and employed so as to increase still further the annual produce.

If the exchangeable value of the annual produce, on the contrary, falls short of the annual consumption, the capital of the society must annually decay in proportion to this deficiency. The expense of the society, in this case, exceeds its revenue, and necessarily encroaches upon its capital. Its capital, therefore, must necessarily decay, and, together with it, the exchangeable value of the annual produce of its industry.*

The balance of produce and consumption is entirely different from what is called the balance of trade. It might take place in a nation which had no foreign trade, but which was entirely separate from all the world. It may take place in the whole globe of the earth, of which the wealth, population, and improvement, may be either gradually increasing or gradually decaying.

The balance of produce and consumption may be constantly in favor of a nation, though what is called the balance of trade be generally against it.

There is nothing Smith says here that does not apply with equal force to the 21st century as the 18th. Even Smith's mockery of the simple-minded mercantilist's

---

* Note that this describes the condition of the United States at the date of publication of this book.

aim of amassing gold and silver hoards reminds us of contemporary mercantilist governments (e.g. China) relentlessly pursuing the dream of bigger and bigger official reserves, this time denominated in dollar, euro, or yen bonds, mere pieces of paper even less intrinsically valuable than yesterday's gold or silver.

Today's trade protectionism, however, often takes a different form than in Smith's day. In the 18th century, the gold standard made it difficult to manipulate a nation's currency value in order to encourage exports and discourage imports. Today currency manipulation is as important as or even more important than traditional trade barriers in protectionist policy-making.

6. Government Subsidies

Crony capitalist alliances between private interests and government do not just restrict or eliminate foreign (or domestic) competition. They also bestow subsidies and other favors upon politically connected industries, a practice which, as Smith says, leads to malinvestment, corruption, and outright "fraud":

> Such payoffs are common enough in prosperous times, but become even more prevalent during downturns. A weak economy gives government a rationale for intervening even more, allegedly in order to fix the economy. As Smith drily notes,

> ... it can very seldom be reasonable to tax the industry of the great body of the people, in order to support that of some particular class of manufacturers.... In public, as well as in private expenses, great wealth, may, perhaps, frequently be admitted as an apology for great folly. But there must surely be something more than ordinary absurdity in continuing such profusion in times of general difficulty and distress.

7. Labor Market Interventions

In Smith's day, the British government had for centuries restricted the mobility of laborers. If you were born in a given locality, you could only move to another with official permission, which was not easy to get. The ostensible purpose of this rule was to avoid vagrancy or the dumping of indigent persons on one locality by another. Its real purpose was to ensure a local supply of labor for rich employers, no matter what the local employment conditions. A side effect of this was to hold back innovation and change in the economy and thus to thwart economic growth.

Government intervention in labor markets has certainly not abated since Smith's day. Today, the black teenage unemployment rate approaches 50%, largely because legislators refuse to exempt teenagers from minimum wage laws. The US federally mandated minimum wag is a bit over $7. But Congress has just passed national medical insurance legislation that will cost employers just under $6 an hour to pay for one employee's family coverage. When this provision comes into effect, the de facto minimum wage for employees with families will almost double, resulting in massive job loss of the very poorest workers.

8. Unintended Consequences as a General Disorder

> Every ... [government economic intervention] ... introduces some degree of real disorder into the constitution of the state, which it will be difficult afterwards to cure without occasioning another disorder.

9. Misdirected Investment

> Every system which endeavors, either, by extraordinary encouragements to draw towards a particular species of industry a greater share of the capital of the society than what would naturally go to it, or, by extraordinary restraints, to force from a particular species of industry some share of the capital which would otherwise be employed in it, is, in reality, subversive of the great purpose which it means to promote. It retards,

instead of accelerating, the progress of the society towards real wealth and greatness; and diminishes, instead of increasing, the real value of the annual produce of its land and labor.

10. Swelling Government Payrolls

The number of public employees increases under the mercantilist (crony capitalist) system, but so does the public pay level:

> The emoluments of offices are not, like those of trades and professions, regulated by the free competition of the market, and do not, therefore, always bear a just proportion to what the nature of the employment requires. They are, perhaps, in most countries, higher than it requires; the persons who have the administration of government being generally disposed to regard both themselves and their immediate dependents, rather more than enough.

11. Out-of-Control Government Spending

> Great nations are never impoverished by private, though they sometimes are by public prodigality and misconduct. The whole or almost the whole, public revenue is, in most countries, employed in maintaining

unproductive hands.... Such people, as they themselves produce nothing, are all maintained by the produce of other men's labor.

It is the highest impertinence and presumption, therefore, in kings and ministers to pretend to watch over the economy of private people, and to restrain their expense, either by sumptuary laws, or by prohibiting the importation of foreign luxuries. They are themselves always, and without any exception, the greatest spendthrifts in the society. Let them look well after their own expense, and they may safely trust private people with theirs. If their own extravagance does not ruin the state, that of the subject never will.

12. High Taxes Contributing to Unemployment

Smith says about taxes in general: "There is no art which one government sooner learns of another, than that of draining the pockets of the people."[118] But public officials give relatively little thought to how taxes may affect employment, an oversight which ultimately hurts government revenue as well as the unemployed:

If direct taxes upon the wages of labor have not always occasioned a proportionable rise in those wages, it is because they have generally occasioned a considerable fall in the demand of labor [i.e. unemployment]. The declension of industry, the decrease of employment for the poor, the diminution of the annual produce of the land and labor of the country, have generally been the effects of such taxes.

In consequence of them, also, the price of labor must always be higher than it otherwise would have been in the actual state of the demand; and this enhancement of price, together with the profit of those who advance it, must always be finally paid by the landlords and consumers. Absurd and destructive as such taxes are, ... they take place in many countries.

The observation of Sir Matthew Decker, that certain taxes are, in the price of certain goods, sometimes repeated and accumulated four or five times, is perfectly just with regard to taxes upon the necessaries of life. In the price of leather, for example, you must pay not only for the tax upon the leather of your own shoes, but for a part of that upon those of the shoemaker and the tanner. You must pay, too, for the tax upon the salt, upon the soap, and upon the candles which those workmen consume while employed in your service; and for the tax upon the leather, which the salt maker, the soap maker, and the candle maker consume, while employed in their service.

In Great Britain, the principal taxes upon the necessaries of life are those upon the four commodities just now mentioned, salt, leather, soap, and candles.

As all those four commodities are real necessaries of life, such heavy taxes upon them must increase somewhat the expense of the sober and industrious poor, and must consequently raise more or less the wages of their labor... [, thereby causing unemployment with no offsetting benefit to them].

The duties of customs are . . . ancient. They seem to have been called customs, as denoting customary payments, [and] . . . appear to have been originally considered as taxes upon the profits of merchants. In those ignorant times, it was not understood, that the profits of merchants are a subject not taxable directly; or that the final payment of all such taxes must fall, with a considerable overcharge, upon the consumers.

13. Debasement of the Currency

In earlier times, impecunious governments often simply seized private property. As Smith noted, this had a particularly chilling effect on economic activity:

> In those unfortunate countries, indeed, where men are continually afraid of the violence of their superiors, they frequently bury or conceal a great part of their stock, in order to have it always at hand to carry with them to some place of safety, in case of their being threatened with any of those disasters to which they consider themselves at all times exposed. This is said to be a common practice in Turkey, in Indostan, and, I believe, in most other governments of Asia.
>
> It seems to have been a common practice among our ancestors during the violence of the feudal government. Treasure-trove was, in these times, considered, as no contemptible part of the revenue of the greatest sovereigns in Europe. It consisted in such treasure as was found concealed in the earth.

Modern governments have adopted more sophisticated means of raising revenue in addition to what can be collected in taxes. If they can find creditors, they borrow. Often the funds are repaid; sometimes they are not.

When national debts have once been accumulated to a certain degree, there is scarce, I believe, a single instance of their having been fairly and completely paid. The liberation of the public revenue, if it has ever been brought about at all, has always been brought about by a bankruptcy; sometimes by an avowed one, through frequently by a pretended payment.

"Pretended payment" refers to debasing the currency:

In every country of the world, I believe, the avarice and injustice of princes and sovereign states, abusing the confidence of their subjects, have by degrees diminished the real quantity of metal, which had been originally contained in their coins. The Roman As, in the latter ages of the Republic, was reduced to the twenty-fourth part of its original value, and, instead of weighing a pound, came to weigh only half an ounce.

The English pound and penny contain at present about a third only; the Scots pound and penny about a thirty-sixth; and the French pound and penny about a sixty-sixth part of their original value.

By means of those operations, the princes and sovereign states which performed them were enabled, in appearance, to pay their debts and fulfill their engagements with a smaller quantity of silver than would otherwise have been requisite. It was indeed in appearance only; for their creditors were really defrauded of a part of what was due to them. All other debtors in the state were allowed the same privilege, and might pay with the same nominal sum of the new and debased coin whatever they had borrowed in the old. Such operations, therefore, have always proved favorable to the debtor, and ruinous to the creditor.

The raising of the denomination of the coin has been [another] expedient by which a real public bankruptcy has been disguised under the appearance of a pretended payment. If a sixpence, for example, should, either by act of parliament or royal proclamation, be raised to the denomination of a shilling, and twenty sixpences to that of a pound sterling; the person who, under the old denomination, had borrowed twenty shillings, or near four ounces of silver, would, under the new, pay with twenty sixpences, or with something less than two ounces.

> A national debt of about a hundred and twenty-eight millions, near the capital of the funded and unfunded debt of Great Britain, might, in this manner, be paid with about sixty-four millions of our present money. It would, indeed, be a pretended payment only, and the creditors of the public would really be defrauded of ten shillings in the pound of what was due to them.

In some later instances, governments dispensed with metal money entirely, and financed themselves with paper. Both the US and Confederate governments did this during their War, and it led directly to runaway inflation. The German government famously did the same in the 1920s, with even greater inflation. Many other governments have done the same since, including the government of the Soviet Union in its final days, and most infamously the government of Zimbabwe.

During the 1920s, government central bankers learned how to create new money without even printing bills through so-called open market operations,[119] and this has become the preferred method in developed nations. Since the 1990s, larger and larger amounts of new money have been surreptitiously "printed" by world governments, partly to pay expenses, but more often to manipulate currency values. The new money led directly to bubbles, thence to the global Crash of 2008, which in turn

Smith put his view of the proper role of government even more succinctly in one of his early university lectures:

> Little else is requisite to carry a state to the highest degree of opulence from the lowest barbarism, but peace, easy taxes, and a tolerable administration of justice: all the rest being brought about by the natural course of things.[120]

15. Muddling through (at Unnecessary Cost to the Poor and Struggling)

Throughout most of human history, the efforts of individuals to better their condition went nowhere. There was little or no economic growth from generation to generation. This fact testified to just how bad governments were, because, in Smith's view, it is difficult to render completely futile the efforts of human enterprise. As he says:

> The natural effort which every man is continually making to better his own condition is a principle of preservation capable of preventing and correcting, in many respects, the bad effects of a political economy, in some degree both partial and oppressive. Such a political economy, though it no doubt retards more or less, is not always capable of

stopping altogether, the natural progress of a nation towards wealth and prosperity, and still less of making it go backwards. If a nation could not prosper without the enjoyment of perfect liberty and perfect justice, there is not in the world a nation which could ever have prospered.

The natural effort of every individual to better his own condition, when suffered to exert itself with freedom and security is so powerful a principle that it is alone, and without any assistance, not only capable of carrying on the society to wealth and prosperity, but of surmounting a hundred impertinent obstructions with which the folly of human laws too often encumbers its operations; though the effect of these obstructions is always more or less either to encroach upon its freedom, or to diminish its security. In Great Britain industry is perfectly secure; and though it is far from being perfectly free, it is as free as or freer than in any other part of Europe.[121]

The signal achievement of *The Wealth of Nations* is to describe mercantilism/crony capitalism both as a whole and in telling detail. As explained earlier, Smith is first and foremost a reformer, and his principal job is to explain the true costs of a corrupt system. But as a reformer, he is also concerned with providing a remedy, which he calls the System of Liberty, and which, we today call free markets:

> [When government relinquishes control of the economy, with all its unintended and damaging consequences,] the obvious and simple system of natural liberty establishes itself of its own accord. Every man, as long as he does not violate the laws of justice, is left perfectly free to pursue his own interest his own way, and to bring both his industry and capital into competition with those of any other man, or order of men.

> The sovereign is completely discharged from a duty, in the attempting to perform which he must always be exposed to innumerable delusions, and for the proper performance of which, no human wisdom or knowledge could ever be sufficient; the duty of superintending the industry of private people, and of directing it towards the employments most suitable to the interests of the society.

Smith's System of Liberty also has its central characteristics.

A. Reliance on Free Prices

Free markets are often described by their critics as both chaotic and wasteful. They are actually both orderly and productive, but only if prices are allowed to be free. Prices are an indispensable signaling device that tells all the economic players what they need to know in order to make rational (and useful) choices.

It has often been observed that the Soviet Union collapsed because it could not find a workable alternative to the free price system. But this is not just a problem for Communist systems. In the so-called market economics of today, all the biggest prices (e.g. currencies, interest rates, mortgage rates) are controlled by government and many of the lesser ones as well.

B. Reliance on Profits

Profits are a corollary of free prices, and are indispensable regulating as well as signaling devices. Of course, we must be careful to describe the profit system accurately as the profit and loss system. The fear and pain of loss counts for as much as or more than the hope for gain.

It is sometimes alleged that the profit system makes goods more expensive, because profit is an "avoidable cost" that is simply tacked on to unavoidable costs such as labor. The truth is that profits are the whip that continually drives prices down, because high prices

> If the prodigality of some were not compen-
> sated by the frugality of others, the conduct
> of every prodigal, by feeding the idle with
> the bread of the industrious, would tend
> not only to beggar himself, but to impov-
> erish his country.

E. An Equivocal View of the Rich

Smith generally takes a jaundiced and critical view of
the rich. He says that

> with the greater part of rich people, the chief
> enjoyment of riches consists in the parade of
> riches; which, in their eye, is never so com-
> plete as when they appear to possess those
> decisive marks of opulence which nobody
> can possess but themselves.

But he does recognize that they have a special role to
play as savers, because unlike most people, the truly rich
simply cannot spend all their income, and thus must save.
And insofar as they are business owners, their

> natural selfishness and rapacity[122]

is regulated by their very desire for profit:

> The real and effectual discipline which is ex-
> ercised over [an employer or other economic
> actor] is not that of [outside parties, including

government], but that of his customers. It is the fear of losing their employment which restrains his frauds and corrects his negligence.

F. Reliance on Enlightened Self-Interest as the Chief Economic Motivator

Not surprisingly, the following are some of the most frequently cited passages of *The Wealth of Nations*:

[The] division of labor, from which so many advantages are derived, is not originally the effect of any human wisdom, which foresees and intends that general opulence to which it gives occasion. It is the necessary, though very slow and gradual, consequence of a certain propensity in human nature to truck, barter, and exchange one thing for another.

In civilized society [an individual] stands at all times in need of the cooperation and assistance of great multitudes, while his whole life is scarce sufficient to gain the friendship of a few persons. It is in vain for him to expect . . . [assistance] . . . from [the] benevolence [of others] only. He will be more likely to prevail if he can interest their self-love in his favor, and show them that it is for their own advantage to do for him what he requires of them.

It is not from the benevolence of the butcher, the brewer, or the baker, that we expect our dinner, but from their regard to their own interest. We address ourselves, not to their humanity, but to their self-love, and never talk to them of our own necessities, but of their advantages.

Every individual is continually exerting himself to find out the most advantageous employment for whatever capital he can command. It is his own advantage, indeed, and not that of the society, which he has in view. But the study of his own advantage naturally, or rather necessarily, leads him to prefer that employment which is most advantageous to the society.

As every individual, therefore, endeavors as much as he can, both to employ his capital in the support of domestic industry, and so to direct that industry that its produce may be of the greatest value; every individual necessarily labors to render the annual revenue of the society as great as he can. He generally, indeed, neither intends to promote the public interest, nor knows how much he is promoting it.

By preferring the support of domestic to that of foreign industry, he intends only his own security; and by directing that industry in such a manner as its produce may be of the greatest value, he intends only his own gain; and he is in this, as in many other cases, led by an invisible hand to promote an end which was no part of his intention.

Nor is it always the worse for the society that it was no part of it. By pursuing his own interest, he frequently promotes that of the society more effectually than when he really intends to promote it. I have never known much good done by those who affected to trade for the public good. It is an affectation, indeed, not very common among merchants, and very few words need be employed in dissuading them from it.

The species of domestic industry which his capital can employ, and of which the produce is likely to be of the greatest value, every individual, it is evident, can in his local situation judge much better than any statesman or lawgiver can do for him. The statesman, who should attempt to direct private people in what manner they ought to employ their capitals, would not only

> load himself with a most unnecessary atten-
> tion, but assume an authority which could
> safely be trusted, not only to no single per-
> son, but to no council or senate whatever,
> and which would nowhere be so danger-
> ous as in the hands of a man who had folly
> and presumption enough to fancy himself
> fit to exercise it.

Smith has sometimes been dismissed as a proponent, even a salesman, of selfishness. This is false. In his first book, *The Theory of Moral Sympathy*, Smith says that human beings are often moved to altruism by what he calls sympathy (we might call it empathy), which he clearly regards in a very positive light.

At the very least, Smith wants our self-interest to be rational and enlightened. He is well aware of how irrational self-interest can be and how it has torn societies asunder and kept them poor. The main point here is that no amount of human goodwill or altruism will create the orderly webs of cooperation that we all need in order to survive. Nor will a command and control system, led from the top by government, even a more honest government than we actually get, succeed.

It is only free markets, pitifully hampered and constrained as they have been by misguided government interventions, which have got us as far as we have come, by channeling our aggressions away from violence and theft and toward constructive enterprise.

And it is free markets alone which offer any hope of eliminating poverty in an environmentally and economically sustainable way.

By emphasizing enlightened self-interest, Smith was no doubt being a realist, and no doubt making an important point. But as this author argued in *Are the Rich Necessary?*, self-interest—even enlightened self-interest—is over-emphasized. The gist of the argument is that the private market system is not fundamentally grounded in self-interest:

> Adam Smith seriously erred in suggesting that it was, and his authority has misled us for centuries. The market system teaches naturally selfish people to put aside their selfishness and practice some of the "highest" values of social cooperation that human beings have ever achieved.

> "Market values" are the diametrical opposite of "every man for himself." The "self-interest model" so beloved of economists is completely illusory. A young person may proclaim: "I will start my own business in order to be my own boss." But if he or she persists in this illusion, the new business will fail, as most do. In order to start and run a successful business, one must be willing, above all, to subordinate oneself in the service of

others. One must serve one's customers and one must also serve and respect and nurture one's employees.

Sometimes "bosses" are so talented or lucky that they do well without fully learning these lessons. Even then, they do not do nearly as well as they might have. The iron rule is: everything else being equal, the better you serve, the better you do. Predation, exploitation, parasitism, or greed may make this transaction, or even this year's profits, fatter. But a business is defined as the present value of all future profits, and these true profits are ruined by selfishness, even so-called "rational" selfishness.

"Market" values are not easy. They are extremely demanding, and in many cases take generations to learn. Nor are they "lower than" or "separate from" religious values. It is true they are not identical to religious values, but they are rather "complementary" to religion and have arguably done as much as religion to "civilize" us, especially given the dark side of religion exemplified by religious wars. It is no coincidence that it was defenders of free markets who led the battle against world slavery and finally won it,

against large odds, in the nineteenth century. As economist George Stigler writes:

> Important as the moral influences of
> the market place are, they have not
> been subjected to any real study. The
> immense proliferation of general ed-
> ucation, of scientific progress, and of
> democracy are all coincidental in time
> and place with the emergence of the
> free enterprise system of organizing
> the market place. I believe this coin-
> cidence was not accidental.[123]

The hostile attitude of most economists toward the idea of the market as a source of
moral values is hard to fathom, although
it may simply reflect a lack of personal fa-
miliarity with business. Listen to Geoffrey
Martin Hodgson:

> The firm has to compete not simply
> for profit but for our confidence and
> trust. To achieve this, it has to abandon
> profit-maximization, or even share-
> holder satisfaction, as the exclusive
> objectives of the organization.[124]

This is quite wrong. In truth, confidence
and trust do not in the least conflict with
profits. On the contrary, one cannot have

the latter without the former, as great businesses have shown throughout history.

G. Honest Money

It may be debated whether Smith over-emphasized
rational self-interest. It may also be debated whether he
got government monetary policy right. This author for
one thinks he got it mostly wrong. Given that monetary
policy has had such a large impact on economic affairs
since his day, and also given Smith's immense authority,
it is worth taking a moment to consider what exactly
The Wealth of Nations said about this subject.

In the first place, Smith objects to government-issued
paper money. His argument is sensible:

> The paper currencies of North America con-
> sisted, not in bank notes payable to the bearer
> on demand, but in a government paper, of
> which the payment was not eligible till sev-
> eral years after it was issued; and though
> the colony governments paid no interest
> to the holders of this paper, they declared
> it to be, and in fact rendered it, a legal ten-
> der of payment for the full value for which
> it was issued.

> Allowing the colony security to be per-
> fectly good, a hundred pounds payable fif-
> teen years hence, for example, in a country

where interest is at six per cent, is worth little more than forty pounds ready money. To oblige a creditor, therefore, to accept of this as full payment for a debt of hundred pounds actually paid down in ready money, was an act of such violent injustice, as has scarce, perhaps, been attempted by the government of any other country which pretended to be free. It bears the evident marks of having originally been, what the honest and downright Doctor Douglas assures us it was, a scheme of fraudulent debtors to cheat their creditors.

As suggested above, Smith does not object to paper money issued by banks, assuming it is backed by gold or silver, and that it is restricted and regulated by government:

If bankers are restrained from issuing any circulating bank notes, or notes payable to the bearer, for less than a certain sum; and if they are subjected to the obligation of an immediate and unconditional payment of such bank notes as soon as presented, their trade may, with safety to the public, be rendered in all other respects perfectly free.

He says that these government restrictions are necessary because some banks act foolishly:

> Had every particular banking company al-
> ways understood and attended to its own par-
> ticular interest, the circulation never could
> have been overstocked with paper money.
> But every particular banking company has
> not always understood or attended to its own
> particular interest, and the circulation has fre-
> quently been overstocked with paper money.

It is not, however, just the bankers who are responsible for this problem:

> The over-trading of some bold projectors
> in both parts of the United Kingdom was
> the original cause of this excessive circula-
> tion of paper money.[125]

Smith is aware that calling for government intervention into banking affairs is inconsistent with the rest of
his argument:

> To restrain private people, it may be said,
> from receiving in payment the promissory
> notes of a banker for any sum, whether great
> or small, when they themselves are willing to
> receive them; or, to restrain a banker from
> issuing such notes, when all his neighbors
> are willing to accept of them is a manifest
> violation of that natural liberty, which it is
> the proper business of law not to infringe,

but to support. Such regulations may, no doubt, be considered as in some respect a violation of natural liberty. But those exertions of the natural liberty of a few individuals, which might endanger the security of the whole society, are, and ought to be, restrained by the laws of all governments; of the most free, as well as of the most despotical. The obligation of building party walls, in order to prevent the communication of fire, is a violation of natural liberty, exactly of the same kind with the regulations of the banking trade which are here proposed.

Smith also seems to have rejected the worry that allowing paper bank notes would lead to consumer price inflation:

The increase of paper money, it has been said, by augmenting the quantity, and consequently diminishing the value, of the whole currency, necessarily augments the money price of commodities. But as the quantity of gold and silver, which is taken from the currency, is always equal to the quantity of paper which is added to it, paper money does not necessarily increase the quantity of the whole currency.

Smith adds that it is proper for government to regulate and restrict the interest rates that banks charge:

> In countries where interest is permitted, the law in order to prevent the extortion of usury generally fixes the highest rate which can be taken without incurring a penalty. . . . In a country such as Great Britain, where money is lent to government at three per cent and to private people, upon good security, at four and four-and-a-half, the present legal rate, five per cent is perhaps as proper as any.

There is an acknowledgment that ready access to cheap but fluctuating bank credit poses a special problem for the conservative business operator. If a business can earn 8% on its capital, it can earn a great deal more by augmenting that capital by borrowing at 4%. The extra profits may in turn enable this business, through borrowing, to expand faster than its competitors, cut price, or otherwise drive competitors out of business. The more conservative business may thus feel itself obliged to borrow whether or not it wishes to, and then both imprudent and prudent business may both collapse if credit is suddenly withdrawn.

Since Smith's time, we have witnessed great credit expansions and great collapses. These have become ever more dramatic and more troublesome, and have not been arrested by the creation of government central banks, indeed they appear to have become worse. In our day, banks are no longer able to print their own paper money. But they are able to issue checks, and these checks act as money. So one way or another, both banks and central banks are able to expand and contract both the supply of money in the economy and the availability and terms of credit.*

In Smith's day, there was still a debate about whether banks should be able to lend more than the money that was actually in the vault. It was not at all clear that they could. Banks began as gold and silver warehouses, and other warehouses were not (and are not) permitted to lend more than they hold or to lend at all without the depositor's explicit permission. Eventually, long after Smith's death, it was decided by courts that banks, unlike other warehouses, could do these things, even though this "fractional reserve banking system" expanded and contracted both money and credit in an unpredictable and often erratic way, which in turn contributed to economic booms and busts.

Unaccountably, Smith is mostly silent about all this. He seems to excuse loose credit, so long as it is regulated by government, even though elsewhere he argues that government regulation cannot work, and

---

* For a more complete explanation of how this works see Hunter Lewis, *Are the Rich Necessary?* (Mt. Jackson, VA: Axios Press, 2009), 303.

that government, being chronically short of funds, will adopt every furtive and destructive device to fund itself. If government cannot be trusted to impose honest taxes or rein in its borrowing, how can government be entrusted with control of the entire money and lending system? No wonder that some contemporary free market economists are so critical of Smith.

The Wealth of Nations also argued that

> the quantity of money . . . must in every country naturally increase as the value of the annual produce increases. The value of the consumable goods annually circulated within the society being greater, will require a greater quantity of money to circulate them.

This proposition may seem reasonable, but actually needs a second look. There is no empirical evidence that additional money is needed as an economy expands. If an economy consists of four identical tools and four dollars, the production of four more tools does not require the production of four more dollars. In the first instance, the tools may each be worth $1. In the latter, the price falls to 50¢. In either case, the role of money, which in this case is to make it possible to trade goods, remains unaffected.

Why is Smith's lapse on this point important? Because he himself says that

> no complaint is more common than that
> of a scarcity of money.[126]

He adds that

> the attention of government never was so
> unnecessarily employed, as when directed
> to watch over the preservation or increase
> of the quantity of money in any country.

But, this injunction notwithstanding, the idea that the money supply must continually increase has been one of the prime justifications for government control of money. It was the supposed need for an "elastic currency" that was invoked in order to pass legislation creating the US Federal Reserve Board in 1913. Of course no one at that time imagined how rapidly the new central bank would run the monetary printing presses, especially during the 1920s boom, the dotcom boom of the 1990s, the housing boom that followed, or especially after the Crash of 2008, or that all the new money created would reduce the purchasing power of the dollar over a little less than a century by about 97%.

As economist Ludwig von Mises has noted:

> if one looks at the catastrophic consequences
> of the great paper money inflations, one
> must admit that ... it would be futile to re-
> tort that these catastrophes were brought

about by the improper use which the governments made of the powers that credit money and fiat money placed in their hands and that wise governments would have adopted sounder policies. As money can never be neutral and stable in purchasing power, a government's plans concerning the determination of the quantity of money can never be impartial and fair to all members of society. Whatever a government does in the pursuit of aims to influence the height of purchasing power depends necessarily upon the rulers' personal value judgments. It always furthers the interests of some groups of people at the expense of other groups. It never serves what is called the commonweal or the public welfare. In the field of monetary policies too there is no such thing as a scientific ought.[127]

It must be stressed that what has been characterized here as Smith's monetary errors are debated. This author regards them as disastrous for subsequent economic history. If only, one wonders, Smith had got this right—how much boom and bust and human suffering would have been averted. But conventional opinion in contemporary economics disagrees. It is either not much concerned with Smith's monetary policy, or agrees with it, or excuses it.

There is a consensus among economists about some of Smith's other errors. The notion that

> the most decisive mark of the prosperity of any country is the increase of the number of its inhabitants,

is not correct. The statement that

> the greatest improvements in the productive powers of labor . . . seem to have been the effects of the division of labor,

is only partly correct. Capital accumulation (which Smith embraces) and new technology arguably matter as much. It is worth noting that there is not much said about technology in *The Wealth of Nations*, and nothing at all about the industrial revolution that was taking shape in Britain at the time. Also missing is the role of the entrepreneur, something mentioned by two earlier apostles of free markets, Cantillon and Turgot.

There are more lapses. No one today agrees that agriculture is inherently more productive than manufacturing, or that housing and services do not count at all as productive economic activity.[128] Many economists also disagree with Smith's approval of retaliatory tariffs[129] (tariffs raised to combat others). It might be added that retaliatory tariffs are the kind of loophole that crony capitalist governments and their private interest friends love. Cannot all tariffs, in some way, be characterized as retaliatory?

Smith's most notorious and generally accepted blunder was his theory of what made goods valuable and how they were priced. As we shall see, this blunder mattered a great deal, but first we should let Smith speak for himself on this important subject of economic valuation:

> What are the rules which men naturally observe, in exchanging either money, or [goods]? These rules determine what may be called the exchangeable value of goods.

> The word VALUE, it is to be observed, has two different meanings, one may be called "value in use"; the other, "value in exchange." The things which have the greatest value in use have frequently little or no value in exchange; and, on the contrary, those which have the greatest value in exchange have frequently little or no value in use. Nothing is more useful than water; but it will purchase scarce anything; scarce anything can be had in exchange for it. A diamond, on the contrary, has scarce any value in use; but a very great quantity of other goods may frequently be had in exchange for it.

Every man is rich or poor according to the degree in which we can afford to enjoy the necessaries, conveniences, and amusements of human life. But after the division of labor has once thoroughly taken place, it is but a very small part of these with which a man's own labor can supply him. The far greater part of them he must derive from the labor of other people, and he must be rich or poor according to the quantity of that labor which he can command, or which he can afford to purchase.

The value of any commodity, therefore, to the person who possesses it, and who means not to use or consume it himself, but to exchange it for other commodities, is equal to the quantity of labor which it enables him to purchase or command. Labor therefore, is the real measure of the exchangeable value of all commodities.

As a corollary of this, high or low wages and profit are the causes of high or low price. It is because high or low wages and profit must be paid, in order to bring a particular commodity to market, that its price is high or low.

At all times and places, that is dear which it is difficult to come at, or which it costs much labor to acquire; and that cheap which is to be had easily, or with very little labor. Labor alone, therefore, never varying in its own value, is the ultimate and real standard by which the value of all commodities can at all times and places be estimated and compared. It is their real price; money is their nominal price only.

When the price of any commodity is neither more nor less than what is sufficient to pay the rent of the land, the wages of the labor, and the profits of the stock employed in raising, preparing, and bringing it to market, according to their natural rates, the commodity is then sold for what may be called its natural price.

The actual price, at which any commodity is commonly sold, is called its market price. It may either be above, or below, or exactly the same with its natural price.

The market price of every particular commodity is regulated by the proportion between the quantity which is actually brought to market, and the demand of those who are willing to pay the natural price of the commodity, or the whole value of the rent, labor, and profit, which must be paid in order to bring it thither.

Such people [who pay the price] may be called the effectual demanders, and their demand the effectual demand; since it may be sufficient to effectuate the bringing of the commodity to market. It is different from the absolute demand. A very poor man may be said, in some sense, to have a demand for a coach and six horses; he might like to have it; but his demand is not an effectual demand, as the commodity can never be brought to market in order to satisfy it.

The preceding makes some useful points, but is generally garbled. As economist Joseph Schumpeter and others have noted, it seems to express several different theories of economic pricing: usefulness; labor cost; difficulty of acquisition; embedded rent, labor, and profit; supply and demand—with perhaps an overall emphasis on labor cost.

As noted earlier, Smith's mentor, noted philosopher (and economist) David Hume, read *The Wealth of Nations* during his final illness. He approved highly of it, but at once noted the error on pricing: "If you were at my fireside, I should dispute some of your principles. I cannot think … but that price is determined altogether by the quantity and the demand."[130]

In other words, a product is not worth the labor in it, or even the rent, labor, and expected profit. It is worth whatever someone is willing to pay for it. Moreover, the seller and buyer do not make an equal exchange. The seller values cash more than the product; the buyer the reverse. This is possible because valuation is subjective in nature.

By the late 19th century, approximately a century after Smith, economists had worked all this out. But in the meantime, Karl Marx had seized on Smith's "labor theory of value" to justify an attack on "capitalism." If labor is what makes goods valuable, then workers should not share that value with capitalists. Profit in this view is both unnecessary and illegitimate.

Marx agreed that capital investment and equipment entered into the equation, but these were characterized as labor from the past. He did not attempt to explain why today's laborers deserved emolument from labor of the past, or how any of this squared with the dictum "from each according to his ability, to each according to his need."[131] But insofar as Marx depended on a labor theory of value, it may be said that Marxist communism depended on Smith.

Well, we all make our mistakes. And we cannot choose what others will do with our ideas. The unmistakable truth remains that Adam Smith very much deserves his central place in the pantheon of economic thinkers, not because he got free market theory right, but because he got mercantilism/crony capitalism so unmistakably right.

In Smith's day, as in our day, it is crony capitalism that rules the roost. This is hard on all of us, but especially the poor and disadvantaged. As Smith states, this is a very sorry state of affairs, and we should not accept it. We should lay bare the flaws of the current system and demand reform, just as Smith and our 18th-century forebears did. And we should take special care not to get sidetracked by false panaceas offered by "correctors" of Smith, such as Marx or John Maynard Keynes, precisely because their "corrections" lead in practice to more rather than less crony capitalism.

A Biographical Sketch

Adam Smith was born in Kirkcaldy, Scotland where his father, who died a few months before his birth, had been controller of customs. At age three, he was taken to visit an uncle, where, playing alone, he was seized by a group of "tinkers." Fortunately, this was noticed and after a hot pursuit, the boy was abandoned and recovered. But for this recovery, we might never have had *The Theory of Moral Sentiments*, Smith's first book, or *The Wealth of Nations*.

In 1737, Smith enrolled at the University of Glasgow, where he studied under Hutcheson, who became an important mentor and source of his ideas. In 1740, he went to Oxford, where, appalled by the utter sloth and neglect of students by teachers, he nevertheless stayed seven years. This was followed by two years at home with his mother, Margaret; then a period of three years lecturing in Edinburgh, where he met and became greatly influenced by the philosopher and economist David Hume; then a move back to Glasgow as professor of logic in 1751, which led to the chair of moral philosophy (then incorporating economics) a year later.

Smith remained at Glasgow for almost twelve years. Later, he described it as "by far the most useful, and therefore by far the happiest period of my life."[132] In 1763, four years after the publication of his first book established his name throughout Britain, he was asked to accompany the young Duke of Buccleuch on a continental tour. This was a very lucrative offer, involving a lifetime pension, and Smith decided to resign his professorship.

Smith and the young Duke got along very well. Residence in Paris opened up a new world, including the most famous economist of the day, François Quesnay, as well as Anne-Robert-Jacques Turgot, another exponent of free markets and critic of the dominant mercantilist policies of the day. Two and a half years into the tour, the Duke's younger brother was suddenly murdered in France, and the party returned to Britain.

For ten years beginning in 1766, Smith lived with his mother at Kirkcaldy, engaged in writing *The Wealth of Nations*. He also described this period as one of great happiness. He was able to send the completed work to his close friend David Hume and also to visit him just prior to his death. Smith's attack on mercantilism really took up where Hume had left off in his own economic writing. Smith also published a letter (to W. Strahan, Smith's publisher) describing Hume's last days, a warm tribute to his friend that offended many churchmen, because of Hume's celebrated atheism.

After the publication of *The Wealth of Nations* in 1776, Smith spent two years in London, enjoying the success of his book and increasing fame. In 1778, his reputation, and especially the efforts of the Duke of Buccleuch, secured him the office of Commissioner of Customs in Scotland, a very handsomely remunerated post, and he moved back to Scotland, taking a house with his mother in Edinburgh. Between his new stipend and the continuing pension from the Duke, Smith was now fairly rich, and it is thought that he spent much of it on secret charities.

Smith's mother died in 1784, then two years later, his cousin, Tane Douglas, who also lived with him. Thereafter his health failed, he suffered, and finally died on July 17, 1790. By his will, most of his unpublished manuscripts were burned, but some survived.

Chapter 11

Immanuel Kant

(1724–1804)

HOW SHOULD WE conduct ourselves in life? And where should we look for guidance? Some of the most celebrated answers have come from the German philosopher Immanuel Kant. To begin with the second question, we cannot simply rely on teachers, even those who speak with a voice of authority. They will inevitably disagree, and then how to choose? Personal experience is of undoubted use in telling us how to live. Once we learn not to touch a hot stove, we rarely need another lesson. But as we arrive at a fork in an unknown road, experience cannot tell us where to go, and this is equally true in our moral travels.

inclination to do so. In this case, men preserve their life as duty requires, no doubt, but not because duty requires. . . .

To be beneficent when we can is a duty. And there are many people so sympathetically constituted that, without any other motive of vanity or self-interest, they find pleasure in spreading joy around them and take delight in the satisfaction of others. But I maintain that in such a case an action of this kind, however proper, however amiable it may be, has nevertheless no true moral worth, but is rather on a level with the inclination to honor. . . .

Our second proposition is this: That an action done from duty derives its moral worth, not from what is to be attained by it, but from how it was chosen, and in particular whether the choice was made without reference to personal desire or material ends. . . .

Our third proposition, which follows from the two preceding, I would express thus: Duty is the necessity of acting out of respect for the law. . . . An action done from duty must wholly exclude the influence of inclination and with it every object of the will, so that nothing remains which can determine the will except objectively the law, and subjectively pure respect for this practical law, and consequently the maxim that I should follow this law even to the thwarting of all my inclinations. . . .

But what sort of law is this, which must guide my will, without any regard to the effect expected from it, in order that my will may be called good absolutely and without qualification? It is this: I am never to act otherwise than so that I could will that my maxim should itself become a universal law. This is the general law that serves the will as its principle and must so serve it, if duty is not to be a vain delusion and a chimerical notion. . . .

The shortest way, and an unerring one, to discover whether a lie is consistent with duty, is to ask myself, "Should I be content that my maxim (to extricate myself from difficulty by a false promise) should hold good as a universal law, for myself as well as for others?"; and should I be able to say to myself, "Everyone may make a deceitful promise when he finds himself in a difficulty from which he cannot otherwise extricate himself?"

Then I presently become aware that while I can will the lie, I can by no means will that lying should be a universal law. For with such a law there would be no promises at all, or people would always pay me back in my own coin. Hence my maxim, as soon as it were made a universal law, would necessarily destroy itself.

I do not, therefore, need any far-reaching penetration to discern what I have to do in order that my will may be morally good. Inexperienced in the course of the world, incapable of being prepared for all its contingencies, I only ask myself: Can I will that my maxim should be a universal law? If not, then it must be rejected, not because of a disadvantage accruing from it to myself or even to others, but because it cannot serve as universal legislation, and logic extorts from me immediate respect for such legislation....

Although common men do not conceive this law in such an abstract and universal form, yet they always have it before their eyes and use it as the standard of their decision....

Innocence is indeed a glorious thing; on the other hand, it is easily seduced. On this account even common wisdom, which otherwise consists more in conduct than in knowledge, has need of philosophy, not in order to learn from it, but to secure for its precepts stability and permanence....

We cannot better serve the wishes of those who ridicule all morality as a mere chimera of the human imagination than by conceding to them that notions of duty must be drawn only from experience. To do this is to prepare for those people a certain triumph....

Reason itself, independent of all experience, ordains what ought to take place. Even if there has never been a sincere friend, yet not a whit the less is pure sincerity in friendship required of every man. Prior to all experience, this duty is commanded by reason operating through a priori principles....

The imperative which commands a certain conduct immediately, without having any other purpose to be attained by it, let the consequence be what it may, is categorical. This imperative may also be called that of morality....

There is but one such categorical imperative, namely, this: Act only in such a way as you can will to become a universal law....

This can also be expressed in this form: Act as if the maxim of your action were to become by your will a universal law of nature....

If, then, there is a supreme practical principle that, with respect to the human will, takes the form of a categorical imperative, it must be one that is an end for everyone because it is an *end in itself.* As it constitutes an objective principle, it can serve as a universal practical law. The foundation of this principle is this: rationality is an end for all rational beings because it is an *end in itself.* Every other rational being stands on this same rational ground that holds for me. From this we derive the practical imperative: *So act that you treat humanity, whether in your own person or that of any other, in every case as an end, never only as a means....*

We can now end where we started at the beginning, namely, with the conception of a will unconditionally good. That will is absolutely good which cannot be evil, in other words, whose maxim, if made a universal law, could never contradict itself. This principle, then, is its supreme law: "Act always on such a maxim as you can at the same time will to be a universal law." This is the sole condition under which a will can never contradict itself; such an imperative is categorical. Since the validity of the will as a universal law for possible actions is analogous to the universal connection of the existence of things by general laws, the categorical imperative can also be expressed thus: Act on maxims which can at the same time have for their object themselves as universal laws of nature. Such then is the formula of an absolutely good will. These different ways of expressing the law are just that—they really express the same law. Each implies the other. . . .

Kant's Categorical Imperative is sometimes confused with the Golden Rule. This Rule, which appears in some form in most established world religions, may be expressed as: "Do unto others as you would have them do unto you."* Although there is some similarity with the Categorical Imperative, logicians are correct that there are fundamental differences. An example that has been cited is the case of a masochist. Since he enjoys pain, he might under the Golden Rule argue that it would be right to inflict pain on others.

The preceding example is not meant to denigrate the Golden Rule. It is an extremely important moral concept, one which states emphatically that unrestrained egoism is not an acceptable way of life; that we must live with others; that we must try to be fair to others; and that disregarding this principle will likely lead to results that even the most ardent egoist will not enjoy. The Categorical Imperative further improves on the Golden Rule by offering the universalizability principle, which sadomasochism would clearly fail.

Kant argues that the universalizability principle can and must be applied without any regard for empirical

---

* Christian Bible, Luke 6:13.

circumstances. It is not clear this is correct. It is clearly correct to argue that universalizing murder would be illogical because it would lead to a world in which no one is left to murder. But let's take a less extreme example. What if I ask myself whether it is morally acceptable to live in a mansion? Under today's circumstances, it would not be possible for every human being to live in a mansion: it would require unavailable resources and probably also take up too much of earth's limited space. Under other circumstances, however, such as reduced population or technological advances, perhaps every human being could live in a mansion. Indeed, what is a mansion? The average modern American home would strike most people living today and almost everyone who lived in the past as a mansion.

It may also be argued that universalizability is not quite as clear and complete a concept as Kant thought. When a parent willingly sacrifices his or her life for a child, that is clearly universalizable. It is not an idea that contradicts itself. Moreover, it has further elements of rationality when considered from the point of view of circumstances: the child by definition in all probability has more future years ahead, if its life is preserved, than the parent has to lose.

Let's imagine, however, that you are hiking in the mountains and see a stranger about to fall from a ledge. To rescue the stranger will entail great risk to one's own life. It is not clear that the Categorical Imperative will tell us in this instance what to do.

These caveats aside, the Categorical Imperative is an immense achievement. Its emphasis on intentions over consequences is often contrasted with Jeremy Bentham's *Utilitarianism*, which put the whole emphasis on consequences. *Utilitarianism* leads to odd and unsatisfactory hypothetical choices. Assume, for example, that by killing one innocent person you could save the lives of ten other people. Would you do it? Most mature, moral people would not make this choice. They would feel, and feel strongly, that it is never right to take an innocent life, no matter what the circumstances. Kant reminds us that this principle is logical, and that the competing utilitarian logic can only take us so far before being consumed in self-contradiction.

Biographical Sketch

Immanuel Kant was born in 1724 in Königsberg, then part of Prussia, now in Russia. He remained in the same city his entire life, never married, devoted himself to philosophy, was appointed Professor of Logic and Metaphysics at the University of Königsberg, and wrote innumerable books including the *Critique of Pure Reason* (1781), which became the single most celebrated book in the history of European philosophy; the *Groundwork of the Metaphysics of Morals* (1785), one of the most celebrated works of moral philosophy; the *Critique of Practical Reason* (1788), which expanded on the *Groundwork*; and the *Critique of Judgment* (1790). The only ripple in what otherwise seemed an outwardly uneventful but prodigiously productive career occurred in 1794 when King Friedrich Wilhelm II officially censured Kant for allegedly veering too far from orthodox Christianity in his book of the same year, *Religion within the Limits of Reason Alone*.

Throughout his life and thereafter, Kant was celebrated for his powers of intense concentration on philosophical questions, devotion to routine, and disregard for the outside world. Will Durant recounts how neighbors could set their clocks by Kant's daily walk outside his home, which took place punctually at the same time each afternoon. One day he was allegedly so wrapped up in thought that he forgot to put on a second shoe and thus walked with only one. Whether true or not, the story captures the spirit of one of the most brilliant "absent-minded" geniuses of world history.

Note regarding the quoted material used in this chapter:

Groundwork of the Metaphysics of Morals by Immanuel Kant, an updated version of translation by Thomas Kingsmill Abbott.

Chapter 12

Edward Gibbon

(1737–1794)

E DWARD GIBBON IS best known as the author of the multi-volume *Decline and Fall of the Roman Empire*, a work still read for its wit and style as well as its comprehensive treatment of almost thirteen hundred years of ancient Roman and Byzantine history. This chapter presents the essence of the last two chapters of volume one, which together describe early Christianity and its effect on the Empire. These chapters were read by many as a not very subtle attack on religion, a sensational charge at the time. Gibbon responded that he was in fact a perfectly orthodox believer, but that

> the theologian may indulge the pleasing task of describing Religion as she descended

from Heaven, arrayed in her native pu-
rity. A more melancholy duty is imposed
on the historian. He must discover the in-
evitable mixture of error and corruption,
which she contracted in a long residence
upon earth, among a weak and degener-
ate race of beings.

It no doubt added considerable fuel to the fire that
the author summed up the theme of his great work
as "the triumph of barbarism and religion." And that
he clearly admired the widespread religious tolerance
in the Roman world, which was initially challenged
by the tenets of Judaism and then completely over-
thrown both by Christian beliefs and by exasperated
Roman attempt to extirpate them:

The various modes of worship which prevailed in the Roman world, were all considered by the people, as equally true; by the
philosopher; as equally false; and by the
magistrate, as equally useful.

He added that

toleration produced not only a mutual in-
dulgence, but even religious concord.

Gibbon did not welcome controversy. He preferred
calm and concord in his own life, time to read and

reflect. He tellingly stated that "I never make the mistake of arguing with people for whose opinions I have no respect." and added that his scholarly work "supplied each day, each hour, with a perpetual source of independent and rational pleasure." He was never so happy as when browsing bookshops in London. After the completion of his history in 1787, he wrote:

> I will not dissemble the first emotions of joy on the recovery of my freedom, and, perhaps, the establishment of my fame. But my pride was soon humbled, and a sober melancholy was spread over my mind by the idea that I had taken an everlasting leave of an old and agreeable companion, and that whatsoever might be the future fate of my history, the life of the historian must be short and precarious.

Begun in 1772, with the first volume appearing in 1776 and the last in 1788, the *Decline and Fall of the Roman Empire* required fifteen years to write and twelve to publish. Here is how Gibbon described its original conception, eight years before beginning it:

> . . . I continued my journey . . . to Rome, where I arrived in the beginning of October. My temper is not very susceptible of enthusiasm, and the enthusiasm which I do not feel

I have ever scorned to affect. But, at the distance of twenty-five years, I can neither forget nor express the strong emotions which agitated my mind as I first approached and entered the *eternal city*. After a sleepless night, I trod, with a lofty step, the ruins of the Forum; each memorable spot where Romulus stood, or Tully spoke, or Caesar fell, was at once present to my eye; and several days of intoxication were lost or enjoyed before I could descend to a cool and minute investigation.... It was at Rome, on the 15th of October, 1764, as I sat musing amidst the ruins of the Capitol, while the barefooted friars were singing vespers in the Temple of Jupiter, that the idea of writing the decline and fall of the city first started to my mind. But my original plan was circumscribed to the decay of the city rather than of the empire: and, though my reading and reflections began to point towards that object, some years elapsed, and several avocations intervened, before I was seriously engaged in the execution of that laborious work.

Gibbon's grandfather had made a fortune, and this inheritance gave him the leisure to choose his own pursuits. British society of the day included notable thinkers such as Samuel Johnson and David Hume, the latter a particular admirer, but upper class and court circles were anything but intellectually inclined. Legend has it that Gibbon brought round a copy of the second volume of his work to present to the Duke of Gloucester, brother of King George III, and was greeted with: "Another d-mn'd thick, square book! Always, scribble, scribble, scribble! Eh! Mr. Gibbon?" Other accounts attribute this remark to the Duke of Cumberland when he encountered Gibbon writing in the garden of a hotel in Europe.

Gibbon's accomplishments are all the more remarkable given the details of his personal life. The eldest of seven children, six of whom died before reaching adulthood, in his own childhood he was in continual poor health and nearly died several times. Neither parent paid much attention to him, perhaps from a belief he would die too. His mother, Judith, herself died when he was ten, and his father left London, with the result that he was largely raised by an aunt, Catharine Porten, who encouraged his reading and to whom he was very devoted.

The man who became a commanding intellectual presence in Europe was only five feet tall and in later life had trouble controlling his weight, partly from physical inactivity. There is a story that he was staying at an English country house for the weekend and on departure found that his hat was missing. He was puzzled because he had not once stepped foot out of doors while there.

moving back to Switzerland. There he shared a house belonging to his friend Deyverdun, which had a garden and lovely views overlooking Lake Lausanne. As Gibbon remarked about the reduction in his income: "I am indeed rich, since my income is superior to my expenses, and my expense is equal to my wishes." In Lausanne, Gibbon found the time to complete his history, which he then brought back to London for publication. Returning to Lausanne in 1789, his happiness was dimmed by the death of Deyverdun. Ill health brought him back again to London in 1793 and he died, either of natural causes or of his treatments, in 1794.

Gibbon's personal and political reflections continue to resonate. About himself, he said: "We improve ourselves by victories over ourself. There must be contests, and you must win." About societies, he said: "All that is human must retrograde if it does not advance." And also: "Our sympathy [as human beings] is cold to the relation of distant misery." About history and politics, his cool, ironic tone, embedded in a majestic style of writing that has often been imitated but never quite duplicated, is particularly memorable:

> . . . The reign of Antoninus is marked by the rare advantage of furnishing very few materials for history, which is indeed little more than the register of the crimes, follies, and misfortunes of mankind.

... [About ancient Athens]: In the end, more than freedom, they wanted security. They wanted a comfortable life, and they lost it all—security, comfort, and freedom. When the Athenians finally wanted not to give to society but for society to give to them, when the freedom they wished for most was freedom from responsibility, then Athens ceased to be free and was never free again.

... The wisdom and authority of the legislator are seldom victorious in a contest with the vigilant dexterity of private interest.

About the relative merits of Roman paganism, ancient Roman philosophy, and early Christianity, Gibbon had many observations, and he offered them more freely than one might have expected, given the age in which he lived and his desire not to engage in pitched battles with outraged Christian clerics or endanger his standing as a member of the British political establishment.

Chapter 13

Jeremy Bentham*

(1748–1832)

ON A SEPTEMBER evening in 1938, the celebrated economist John Maynard Keynes (1883–1946) lay draped over a favorite chaise longue in the double drawing room of his London townhouse. He was surrounded by intimate friends of several generations who gathered periodically to share memoirs and who referred to themselves as the "memoir club." The spirit of the gathering is suggested by Keynes's opening remarks:

---

* This chapter represents a revised and expanded version of material that was first published in Hunter Lewis, *A Question of Values: Six Ways We Make The Personal Choices That Shape Our Lives* (San Francisco: Harper Collins, 1990).

If it will not shock the club too much, I should like in this contribution to its proceedings to introduce for once, mental or spiritual, instead of sexual, adventures, to try—and recall the principal impacts on one's virgin mind and to wonder how it has all turned out.

He continued as follows in what was later published as an essay titled "My Early Beliefs":

I went up to Cambridge at Michaelmas 1902, and Moore's *Principia Ethica* came out at the end of my first year. . . . It was exciting, exhilarating, the beginning of a renaissance, the opening of a new heaven on a new earth. . . .

Even if the new members of the Club know what [this new] religion was it will not do any of us any harm to try and recall the crude outlines. Nothing mattered except states of mind. . . . These states of mind were not associated with action or achievement or with consequences. They consisted in timeless, passionate states of contemplation and communion. . . . The appropriate subjects of passionate contemplation and communion were a beloved person, beauty and truth, and one's prime objects in life were love, the creation and enjoyment of aesthetic experience, and the pursuit of knowledge. Of these love came a long way first. . . .

Our religion was altogether unworldly—with wealth, power, popularity, or success it had no concern whatever, they were thoroughly despised.

This religion . . . is still my religion under the surface. . . .

The fundamental intuitions of *Principia Ethica* . . . brought us one big advantage. . . . We were amongst the first of our generation . . . to escape from the Benthamite tradition. . . . I do now regard that as the worm which has been gnawing at the insides of modern civilization and is responsible for its present moral decay. We used to regard the Christians as the enemy, because they appeared as the representatives of tradition, convention, and hocus-pocus. In truth it was the Benthamite calculus, based on an over-valuation of the economic criterion, which was destroying the quality of the popular Ideal.[132]

Throughout his life, Keynes had an ambivalent relationship with Moore's aim of transcending worldly

> I would have the dearest friend I have to know
> that his interests, if they come in competi-
> tion with those of the public, are as noth-
> ing to me. Thus I would serve my friends—
> thus would I be served by them.[134]

The inventor of this remarkable doctrine, which lit-
erally stood Christianity on its head by deriving goodness and altruism from pleasure and materialism, was
one of a long line of English eccentrics. A graduate of
Oxford at fifteen and an obsessive toiler at dry-as-dust
tracts on law, penology, economics, and public sanitation, as well as on philosophy, he was too shy to publish anything. His friends had to purloin his manuscripts and secretly publish them—with the result that
the wealthy recluse unwittingly became a public figure, a hugely successful reformer, and one of the most
influential philosophers of all time.

In typical fashion, Bentham worried about making
his death as useful as possible and directed that his body
should be publicly dissected. Subsequently, his face
was reconstructed with wax, his skeleton clothed in a
respectable dark suit, and his visible remains placed on
permanent display at University College, Cambridge.

The year that Bentham died, one of his chief pro-
tégés, John Stuart Mill, was only twenty-six years old.
Educated by a father who thought that "life [was]
a poor thing at best, after the freshness of youth and
of unsatisfied curiosity had gone by," by age three he

had begun to read ancient Greek; by sixteen he had adopted the term utilitarianism to describe his own and Bentham's philosophy; by twenty-one, he had suffered a devastating nervous breakdown, a breakdown that was forever after cited by proponents of "natural" and "unstressed" child rearing.

In subsequent years, Mill softened (or, as some would say, muddled) Benthamite utilitarianism by distinguishing between so-called higher and lower pleasures: "It is better to be a human being dissatisfied than a pig satisfied; better to be Socrates dissatisfied than a fool satisfied."[135] He also proposed a "rule utilitarianism" in which we consider the consequences of following a general rule as opposed to "act utilitarianism" in which we consider the consequences of a particular act. The advantage of following a rule is that the odds of knowing the likely consequences are greater, although there always must be exceptions to the rule as we contemplate the act.

Various thinkers have gotten lost in the weeds here. When driving a car, is the rule to stay on the right side of the road?—in which case the rule does not work in Britain. Or is the rule simply to follow traffic laws, in which case it works both places. Philosopher David Lyons (b. 1935) argues that there is no real difference between "rule" and "act" utilitarianism, but he does not appear to be correct about this. The "rule" approach is much easier to follow.

Mill also attempted, as Bentham never had, to supply a logical proof for the proposition (deduction) that happiness can be equated with pleasure. Mill's proof, in turn, had its critics. As Bertrand Russell, later remarked:

> [Mill says]: Pleasure is the only thing desired; therefore pleasure is the only thing desirable. He argues that the only things visible are things seen, the only things audible are things heard, and similarly the only things desirable are things desired. He does not notice that a thing is "visible" if it can be seen, but "desirable" if it ought to be desired.

Russell thus in effect reiterated David Hume's dictum that an "ought" is logically separate (and cannot be derived) from an "is," a subject that we discussed in the introduction and in the chapter on Hume. Whether or not an "ought" actually can be derived from an "is," neither Mill nor Bentham demonstrated that their "ought" could be so derived.[136] On a less theoretical level, there have been numerous objections to Bentham and Mill's ideas. When we refuse to murder five in order to spare the lives of ten people, we are rejecting the core Benthamite principle that results for the majority trump anything else, that minority rights do not exist. Moreover, we almost never know with absolute certainty what the results will be, although a rule helps, and may not even agree about whether the most likely results are desirable. What if the five people whose lives will be sacrificed are all saints while the ten to be spared are all Nazis? And how can we be sure they are Nazis? Jesus and Hitler cannot be expected to use the Benthamite calculus in the same way or arrive at anything like the same result, even if they endorsed its use. The idea that the end might justify the means has by now been thoroughly discredited by 20th-century "reformers" like Mao, Lenin, Stalin, or Pol Pot who ended up murdering so many millions.

At the same time, some of the ideas Bentham promoted have a long history and continue to have much to teach us. It was Epicurus who first noted that human beings prefer pleasure to pain; Francis Hutcheson (1694–1746) observed that the number of people affected by a decision made a great deal of difference. Michel de Montaigne introduced or at least employed the term utility in his "Essay On Experience." David Hume also employed it and used it to stress the importance not just of motive, but of consequence. Bentham was familiar with all of these thinkers and was building on their ideas.

It is not uncommon for contemporary moral philosophers to call themselves utilitarians in the sense of judging consequences to be very important indeed. There is still a kind of popular "religion of usefulness," of striving to make oneself useful to others, which echoes the great philosopher. We must not forget that Bentham himself succeeded in making himself very useful. He was a great reformer. He reformed laws, penal codes, and in general worked tirelessly to help others and improve conditions in 19th-century Britain. He even campaigned for animal as well as human rights. He instructed us to

> create all the happiness you are able to create; remove all the misery you are able to remove. Every day will allow you—will invite you to add something to the pleasure of others—or to diminish something of their pains. (To a young girl, June 1830)

He also noted that "the rarest of human qualities is consistency," and he himself was very consistent. He followed his own code wherever it took him. It led to most of the British public regarding him as a kind of secular saint, although a very human one who reminded us that "Stretching his hand up to reach the stars, too often man forgets the flowers at his feet." (*Deontology*)

Here are a few more celebrated sayings of Jeremy Bentham's:

> In no instance has a system in regard to religion been ever established, but for the purpose, as well as with the effect of its being made an instrument of intimidation, corruption, and delusion, for the support of depredation and oppression in the hands

of governments. (*Constitutional Code; For the Use of All Nations and All Governments Professing Liberal Opinions, Volume 1*)

No power of government ought to be employed in the endeavor to establish any system or article of belief on the subject of religion. (*Ibid.*)

In the mind of all, fiction, in the logical sense, has been the coin of necessity—in that of poets of amusement—in that of the priest and the lawyer of mischievous immorality in the shape of mischievous ambition—and too often both priest and lawyer have framed or made in part this instrument. (*The Panopticon Writings*)

If a man happen to take it into his head to assassinate with his own hands, or with the sword of justice, those whom he calls heretics, that is, people who think, or perhaps only speak, differently upon a subject which neither party understands, he will be as much inclined to do this at one time as at another. Fanaticism never sleeps: it is never glutted: it is never stopped by philanthropy; for it makes a merit of trampling on philanthropy: it is never stopped by conscience; for it has pressed conscience into its service.

Part Four

Modern Moral Thinkers and Doers

Chapter 14

Jane Addams

(1860–1935)

J ANE ADDAMS WAS arguably the most influential woman in American history. In 1897 she founded Hull House, a "settlement house" intended to serve the poor of Chicago, and lived there the rest of her life.

As time passed, she became a spokesperson for the poor, for women, for children, for families, for sanitation, for public health, for social and political reform, first in Chicago, then nationally, and finally throughout the world. In her time, she was as famous as a president, and her books were read everywhere.

Concern for the poor and minorities led her gradually into active politics. This included, in addition to municipal reform, winning voting rights for women and also a pacifist approach to world affairs. In 1931, she became the first American woman to win the Nobel Peace Prize.

Addams was among the first female American public intellectuals, and a hugely successful activist and reformer as well. Many in her own day and later regarded her, in addition, as a kind of secular saint. Her story shines forth brightly in her inspiring and easy-to-read autobiography.

In her early days, the future "saint" resisted efforts to mold her into a professing Christian, or alternatively, into a socialist. She complained of the "wilderness of dogma."[137] But she did eventually become a member of the Presbyterian Church. At first, on leaving college, she thought she would "study medicine and 'live with the poor.'"[138] She gave up the first ambition, but the second stayed with her during a few years of wandering around Europe with her lifelong friend, companion, and later deputy, Ellen Starr.

A particular incident deepened her resolve. In London she

> saw for the first time the overcrowded quarters of a great city at midnight. A small party of tourists were taken to the East End by a city missionary to witness the Saturday night sale of decaying vegetables and fruit, which, owing to the Sunday laws in London, could not be sold until Monday, and,

as they were beyond safe keeping, were disposed of at auction as late as possible on Saturday night. On Mile End Road, from the top of an omnibus which paused at the end of a dingy street lighted by only occasional flares of gas, we saw two huge masses of ill-clad people clamoring around two hucksters' carts. They were bidding their farthings and ha'pennies for a vegetable held up by the auctioneer, which he at last scornfully flung, with a gibe for its cheapness, to the successful bidder. In the momentary pause only one man detached himself from the groups. He had bidden in a cabbage, and when it struck his hand, he instantly sat down on the curb, tore it with his teeth, and hastily devoured it, unwashed and uncooked as it was. . . . The final impression was not of ragged, tawdry clothing nor of pinched and sallow faces, but of myriads of hands, empty, pathetic, nerveless, and work worn, showing white in the uncertain light of the street, and clutching forward for food which was already unfit to eat. . . .

During her years of finding herself, Addams was often plagued by a variety of illnesses, some related to a congenital back deformity, and by nervous exhaustion. Money she did not lack, because she was the sole heir of a successful, self-made, rural Illinois merchant. But even the question of how to spend and how to invest her fortune posed problems:

> In one of the . . . summers between . . . European journeys I visited a western state where I had formerly invested a sum of money in mortgages. I was much horrified by the wretched conditions among the farmers, which had resulted from a long period of drought, and one forlorn picture was fairly burned into my mind. A number of starved hogs—collateral for a promissory note— were huddled into an open pen. Their backs were humped in a curious, camel-like fashion, and they were devouring one of their own number, the latest victim of absolute starvation or possibly merely the one least able to defend himself against their voracious hunger. The farmer's wife looked on indifferently, a picture of despair as she stood in the door of the bare, crude house, and the two children behind her, whom she vainly tried to keep out of sight, continually thrust forward their faces almost covered by masses of coarse, sunburned hair, and their little bare feet so black, so hard, the great cracks so filled with dust that they looked like flattened hoofs. The children

could not be compared to anything so joyous as satyrs, although they appeared but half-human. It seemed to me quite impossible to receive interest from mortgages placed upon farms which might at any season be reduced to such conditions, and with great inconvenience to my agent and doubtless with hardship to the farmers, as speedily as possible I withdrew all my investment.

In founding Hull House, Addams discovered that her own funds did not go very far. As she coolly notes:

We were often bitterly pressed for money and worried by the prospect of unpaid bills, and we gave up one golden scheme after another because we could not afford it; we cooked the meals and kept the books and washed the windows without a thought of hardship if we thereby saved money for the consummation of some ardently desired undertaking.

Hull House was modeled after Toynbee Hall in London. Each day it opened its doors to mothers leaving children in a nursery, to young and old people coming to classes and social clubs, and to people seeking assistance. As Addams describes it:

The memory of the first years at Hull House is more or less blurred with fatigue, for we

could of course become accustomed only
gradually to the unending activity and to
the confusion of a house constantly filling
and refilling with groups of people.

There were many gratifying successes. Boys kept off
the streets were not arrested for juvenile offenses. Girls
were protected from prostitution rings. An uncar-
ing and unresponsive city bureaucracy was forced to
respond a little more. Deserted wives and bewildered
widows were given some assistance. Recalcitrant phar-
macists were stopped from selling cocaine to minors;
garment sweatshops were stopped from sending out
smallpox infected garments. One of the greatest triumphs was the long drawn out battle to clean up the
fetid streets piled high with garbage and human sew-
age, all of which contributed to a high death toll. As
Addams writes:

Possibly our efforts slightly modified the worst
conditions, but they still remained intolerable, and the fourth summer the situation
became for me absolutely desperate when I
realized in a moment of panic that my delicate little nephew for whom I was guard-
ian, could not be with me at Hull House at
all unless the sickening odors were reduced.
I may well be ashamed that other delicate
children who were torn from their families,

not into boarding school but into eternity, had not long before driven me to effective action. Under the direction of the first man who came as a resident to Hull House, we began a systematic investigation of the city system of garbage collection, both as to its efficiency in other wards and its possible connection with the death rate in the various wards of the city.

The Hull House Woman's Club had been organized the year before by the resident kindergartner who had first inaugurated a mother's meeting. The new members came together, however, in quite a new way that summer when we discussed with them the high death rate so persistent in our ward. After several club meetings devoted to the subject, despite the fact that the death rate rose highest in the congested foreign colonies and not in the streets in which most of the Irish American club women lived, twelve of their number undertook, in connection with the residents, to carefully investigate the conditions of the alleys. During August and September, the substantiated reports of violations of the law sent in from Hull House to the health department were one thousand and thirty-seven. For the club woman who had finished a long day's work of washing or ironing followed by the cooking of a hot supper, it would have been much easier to sit on her doorstep during a summer evening than to go up and down ill-kept alleys and get into trouble with her neighbors over the condition of their garbage boxes. It required both civic enterprise and moral conviction to be willing to do this three evenings a week during the hottest and most uncomfortable months of the year. Nevertheless, a certain number of women persisted, as did the residents, and three city inspectors in succession were transferred from the ward because of unsatisfactory services. Still the death rate remained high and the condition seemed little improved throughout the next winter. In sheer desperation, the following spring when the city contracts were awarded for the removal of garbage, with the backing of two well-known businessmen, I put in a bid for the garbage removal of the nineteenth ward. My paper was thrown out on a technicality but the incident induced the mayor to appoint me the garbage inspector of the ward.

The salary was a thousand dollars a year, and the loss of that political "plum" made a great stir among the politicians. The position was no sinecure whether regarded from the point of view of getting up at six in the morning to see that the men were early at work; or of following the loaded wagons, uneasily dropping their contents at intervals, to their dreary destination at the dump; or of insisting that the contractor must increase the number of his wagons from nine to thirteen and from thirteen to seventeen, although he assured me that he lost money on every one and that the former inspector had let him off with seven; or of taking careless landlords into court because they would not provide the proper garbage receptacles; or of arresting the tenant who tried to make the garbage wagons carry away the contents of his stable.

With the two or three residents who nobly stood by, we set up six of those doleful incinerators which are supposed to burn garbage with the fuel collected in the alley itself. The one factory in town which could utilize old tin cans was a window weight factory, and we deluged that with ten times as many tin cans as it could use—much less would pay for. We made desperate attempts to have the dead animals removed by the contractor who was paid most liberally by the city for that purpose but who, we slowly discovered, always made the police ambulances do the work, delivering the carcasses upon freight cars for shipment to a soap factory in Indiana where they were sold for a good price although the contractor himself was the largest stockholder in the concern.

Careful inspection combined with other causes, brought about a great improvement in the cleanliness and comfort of the neighborhood and one happy day, when the death rate of our ward was found to have dropped from third to seventh in the list of city wards and was so reported to our Woman's Club, the applause which followed recorded the genuine sense of participation in the result, and a public spirit which had "made good."

But the cleanliness of the ward was becoming much too popular to suit our all-powerful alderman and, although we felt fatuously secure under the regime of civil service, he found a way to circumvent us by eliminating the position altogether. He introduced an ordinance into the city council which combined the collection of refuse with the cleaning and repairing of the streets, the whole to be placed under a ward superintendent. The office of course was to be filled under civil service regulations but only men were eligible to the examination. Although this latter regulation was afterwards modified in favor of one woman, it was retained long enough to put the nineteenth ward inspector out of office. . . .

In the summer of 1902 during an epidemic of typhoid fever in which our ward, although containing but one thirty-sixth of the population of the city, registered one-sixth of the total number of deaths, two of the Hull House residents made an investigation of the methods of plumbing in the houses adjacent to conspicuous groups of fever cases.

The agitation finally resulted in a long and stirring trial before the civil service board of half of the employees in the Sanitary Bureau, with the final discharge of eleven out of the entire force of twenty-four. The inspector in our neighborhood was a kindly old man, greatly distressed over the affair, and quite unable to understand why he should have not used his discretion as to the time when a landlord should be forced to put in modern appliances. If he was "very poor," or "just about to sell his place," or "sure that the house would be torn down to make room for a factory," why should one "inconvenience" him? The old man died soon after the trial, feeling persecuted to the very last and not in the least understanding what it was all about. We were amazed at the commercial ramifications which graft in the city hall involved and at the indignation which interference with it produced. Hull House lost some large subscriptions as the result of this investigation, a loss which, if not easy to bear, was at least comprehensible. We also uncovered unexpected graft in connection with the plumbers' unions, and but for the fearless testimony of one of their members, could never have brought the trial to a successful issue.

There were many instances where Addams could do nothing, try as she might. There is the pathetic story of the mother wetting herself at work while her baby starved:

I was detained late one evening in an office building by a prolonged committee meeting of the Board of Education. As I came out at eleven o'clock, I met in the corridor of the fourteenth floor a woman whom I knew, on her knees scrubbing the marble tiling. As she straightened up to greet me, she seemed so wet from her feet up to her chin, that I hastily inquired the cause. Her reply was that she left home at five o'clock every night and had no opportunity for six hours to nurse her baby. Her mother's milk mingled with the very water with which she scrubbed the floors until she should return at midnight, heated and exhausted, to feed her screaming child with what remained within her breasts. . . .

Equally heart rending is the story of "Goosie" and his mother:

I recall . . . the mother of "Goosie," as the children for years called a little boy who, because he was brought to the nursery wrapped up in his mother's shawl, always had his hair filled with the down and small feathers from the feather brush factory where she worked. One March morning, Goosie's mother was hanging out the washing on a shed roof before she left for the factory. Five-year-old Goosie was trotting at her heels handing her clothes pins, when he was suddenly blown off the roof by the high wind into the alley below. His neck was broken by the fall, and as he lay piteous and limp on a pile of frozen refuse, his mother cheerily called him to "climb up again," so confident do over-worked mothers become that their children cannot get hurt. After the funeral, as the poor mother sat in the nursery postponing the moment when she must go back to her empty rooms, I asked her, in a futile effort to be of comfort, if there was anything more we could do for her. The overworked, sorrow-stricken woman looked up and replied, "If you could give me my wages for tomorrow, I would not go to work in the factory at all. I would like to stay at home all day and hold the baby. Goosie was always asking me to take him and I never had any time." This statement revealed the condition of many nursery mothers who are obliged to forego the joys and solaces which belong to even the most poverty-stricken. The long hours of factory labor necessary for earning the support of a child leave no time for the tender care and caressing which may enrich the life of the most piteous baby.

If small children were not left alone in tenements for most of the day, they were often made to work themselves:

The visits we made in the neighborhood constantly discovered women sewing upon sweatshop work, and often they were assisted by incredibly small children. I remember a little girl of four who pulled out basting threads hour after hour, sitting on a stool at the feet of her Bohemian mother, a little bunch of human misery. But even for that there was no legal redress, for the only child-labor law in Illinois, with any provision for enforcement, had been secured by the coal miners' unions, and was confined to children employed in mines.

There was at that time no statistical information on Chicago industrial conditions, and Mrs. Florence Kelley, an early resident of Hull House, suggested to the Illinois State Bureau of Labor that they investigate the sweating system in Chicago with its attendant child labor. The head of the Bureau adopted this suggestion and engaged Mrs. Kelley to make the investigation. When the report was presented to the Illinois Legislature, a special committee was appointed to look into the Chicago conditions. I well recall that on the Sunday the members of this commission came to dine at Hull House, our hopes ran high, and we believed that at last some of the worst ills under which our neighbors were suffering would be brought to an end.

As a result of its investigations, this committee recommended to the Legislature the provisions which afterward became those of the first factory law of Illinois, regulating the sanitary conditions of the sweatshop and fixing fourteen as the age at which a child might be employed.

It was, perhaps, a premature effort, though certainly founded upon a genuine need, to urge that a clause limiting the hours of all women working in factories or workshops to eight a day, or forty-eight a week, should be inserted in the first factory legislation of the State....

The eight-hour clause ... met with much less opposition in the Legislature than was anticipated, and was enforced for a year before it was pronounced unconstitutional by the Supreme Court of Illinois....

So Jane Addams's life went. Two steps forward, one back, all in a ceaseless swirl of activity. She was admired, even lionized. She was also reviled, condemned as a radical or even an anarchist. Later in life, her embrace of the worldwide pacifist movement after World War I, embroiled her in further controversy. But, throughout it all, her reputation, her standing, her fame, just kept spreading, along with her combination of Christian charity with political reform, until she became one of the most celebrated, and one of the most justly celebrated, figures of American history.

Chapter 15

Ludwig von Mises
(1881–1973)

W E HAVE ALREADY discussed in the introduction how economist Ludwig von Mises
built on the work of philosopher and economist David Hume among others and provided many
important new or better articulated insights. Unlike
Hume, von Mises limited himself to economics. He
did not write as a moral philosopher. But his thinking has major implications for moral philosophy as well
as economics.

It is also not at all a stretch to call Mises a secular
saint. He led an exemplary life of service to economics,
to scholarship, to country (Austria, then Switzerland,
and finally the US), and to all of humanity. He faced

tremendous adversity over and over again with courage and aplomb, and never wavered from his commitment to telling the truth, no matter what cost to his career or material fortunes.

Born in what is now the Ukraine, Mises grew up in Austria and became, first a professor at the University of Vienna, and then finance minister of Austria. As a Jew, he would not have survived in Austria and as the Nazis tightened their noose on his homeland, he escaped to Switzerland. In 1940, he succeeded in emigrating to the United States with his wife Margrit but had to abandon all his books and papers. Once in the United States, this internationally renowned and prolific economist had to adjust to writing in English rather than German and faced complete rejection by the economics profession establishment for his opposition to the dominant Anglo-American (Keynesian) ideas of the day, but was able to find some work as an adjunct scholar at the New York University Business School. Thereafter, he continued to live and work in New York City while being ostracized by the luminaries of his own profession. The committee controlling the Nobel Prize in economics in particular refused to acknowledge his work while he was living, but the year after Mises died they gave a shared prize to Mises's student Friedrich Hayek. Since the Nobel can only be given to a living person, it is quite clear that the timing of all this was quite deliberate.

Of his trials and tribulations, Mises himself said:

> How one carries on in the face of unavoidable catastrophe is a matter of temperament. In high school, as was custom, I had chosen a verse by Virgil to be my motto: *Tu ne cede malis sed contra audentior ito.* "Do not give in to evil, but proceed ever more boldly against it." I recalled these words during the darkest hours of the war. Again and again I had met with situations from which rational deliberation found no means of escape; but then the unexpected intervened, and with it came salvation. I would not lose courage even now. I wanted to do everything an economist could do. I would not tire in saying what I knew to be true.... (*Notes and Recollections,* p. 70)

> From time to time I entertained the hope that my writings would bear practical fruit and show the way for policy. I have always looked for evidence of a change.... But I never actually deceived myself; my theories explain, but cannot slow the decline of a great civilization. I set out to be a reformer, but only became the historian of decline.... (*Notes and Recollections,* p. 115)

Mises called his principal approach to economics praxeology, which consists of a logical analysis of human alternatives in order to make the best choices. Although experience counts, logic is the essential tool.

Despite his adopting English late in life, Mises spoke and wrote so clearly that this chapter will mostly allow him to speak in his own words. All of the passages selected can also be found in Mark Thornton's book-length work *The Quotable Mises*, available for free at Mises.org. Most writing since 1923 remains under copyright, but the Mises Institute in Auburn, Alabama, has fortunately obtained most rights and allows unrestricted use.

On the Role of Economics

Mises begins by noting that:

> Economics is not about goods and services; it is about human choice and action. . . .

> Economics must not be relegated to classrooms and statistical offices and must not be left to esoteric circles. It is the philosophy of human life and action and concerns everybody and everything. It is the pith of civilization and of man's human existence. . . .
> (*Human Action,* pp. 874, 878)

> There is economics and there is economic history. The two must never be confused. . . .
> (*Austrian Economics: An Anthology,* p. 155)

The unpopularity of economics is the result of its analysis of the effects of privileges. It is impossible to invalidate the economists' demonstration that all privileges hurt the interests of the rest of the nation or at least a great part of it. . . . (*Austrian Economics: An Anthology*, p. 58)

The main achievement of economics is that it has provided a theory of peaceful human cooperation. . . . (*Economic Freedom and Interventionism*, p. 235)

No very deep knowledge of economics is usually needed for grasping the immediate effects of a measure; but the task of economics is to foretell the remoter effects, and so to allow us to avoid such acts as attempt to remedy a present ill by sowing the seeds of a much greater ill for the future. . . . (*The Theory of Money and Credit*, p. 23)

On Praxeology

Mises's praxeology defines man as an acting being and then draws logical inferences from that description:

What distinguishes the Austrian School and will lend it everlasting fame is its doctrine of economic action, in contrast to one of economic equilibrium or nonaction.... (*Notes and Recollections*, p. 36.)

Human action is purposeful behavior.... (*Human Action*, p. 11)

Human life is an unceasing sequence of single actions.... (*Human Action*, p. 45)

Action ... is not simply behavior, but behavior begot by judgments of value, aiming at a definite end and guided by ideas concerning the suitability or unsuitability of definite means.... It is conscious behavior. It is choosing. It is volition; it is a display of the will.... (*The Ultimate Foundation of Economic Science*, p. 34)

Man thinks not only for the sake of thinking, but also in order to act.... (*Epistemological Problems of Economics*, p. 37)

Action is an attempt to substitute a more satisfactory state of affairs for a less satisfactory one. We call such a willfully induced alteration an exchange. [It is] ... aim[ed] at removing uneasiness.... (*Human Action*, pp. 97, 882)

Most actions do not aim at anybody's defeat or loss. They aim at an improvement in conditions.... (*Human Action,* p. 116)

Economics, as a branch of the more general theory of human action, deals with all human action, i.e., with man's purposive aiming at the attainment of ends chosen, whatever these ends may be.... (*Human Action,* pp. 880, 884)

The Nature of Choice

Our choices are made subjectively, in the sense that each of us chooses how to act. Mises emphasizes this:

All judgments of value are personal and subjective. There are no judgments of value other than those asserting *I* prefer, *I* like better, *I* wish.... (*Theory and History,* p. 22)

Value is not intrinsic, it is not in things. It is within us; it is the way in which man reacts to the conditions of his environment. Neither is value in words and doctrines, it is reflected in human conduct. It is not what a man or groups of men say about value that counts, but how they act.... (*Human Action,* p. 96)

A judgment of value does not measure, it arranges in a scale of degrees, it grades. It is expressive of an order of preference and sequence, but not expressive of measure and weight..... (*Human Action,* p. 97)

It is vain to speak of any calculation of values ... [or] a unit of value. ... Calculation is possible only with cardinal numbers. The difference between the valuation of two states of affairs is entirely psychical and personal. ... It cannot be communicated or imparted [through ordinal numbers] to any fellow man. ... (*Human Action,* pp. 97, 205-6)

So far, one may clearly understand that Mises is a subjectivist. He states that our choices are made subjectively, that is, according to how each one of us sees the world. But it is not so simple. We may make our own choices but they must be realistic choices if we are to have the slightest chance of success in achieving whatever it is we want. We must either face reality or face the consequences. We are not living in a Garden of Eden.

The Limits of Subjectivity

In nature there is nothing that could be called freedom. Nature is inexorable necessity. ... (*Planning for Freedom,* p. 215)

In nature there prevail irreconcilable conflicts of interest. The means of subsistence are scarce. Proliferation tends to outrun subsistence. Only the fittest plants and animals survive. The antagonism between an animal starving to death and another that snatches the food away from it is implacable.... (*Human Action,* pp. 273–74)

Nature is not bountiful but stingy. It has restricted the supply of all things indispensable for the preservation of human life. It has populated the world with animals and plants to whom the impulse to destroy human life and welfare is in wrought. It displays powers and elements whose operation is damaging to human life and to human endeavors to preserve it. Man's survival and well-being are an achievement of the skill with which he has utilized the main instrument with which nature has equipped him—reason.... (*The Anti-Capitalistic Mentality,* p. 81)

However we might like it to be otherwise, we cannot refuse to accept the world in which we live and its cause and effect imperatives. These are tremendous constraints and they are objective, not subjective, not subject to our wishes and fantasies. We not only have physical limitations in an often challenging world. We have severe mental limitations. And we generally cannot accomplish anything alone. We must accept the objective constraint of what other people want and under what circumstances they will or will not help us. All of this is very complicated, so much so that we need to develop rules that will help us make the best of what would otherwise be, in Thomas Hobbes's famous phrase, a "nasty, brutish, and short" life.

Even time is a major constraint for us. We do not just need food. We need it now. Or conversely, we do not need it now, we need it next winter, when it will no longer be generally available. Everything is bounded by time in some way:

> Man is subject to the passing of time. He comes into existence, grows, becomes old, and passes away. His time is scarce. He must economize it as he economizes other scarce factors.... (*Human Action,* p. 101)

> Man's striving after an improvement of the conditions of his existence impels him to action [within some specified timeframe]. Action requires planning and the decision which of various plans is the most advantageous.... (*The Ultimate Foundation of Economic Science,* p. 90)

> Man is not, like the animals, an obsequious puppet of instincts and sensual impulses.

> Man has the power to suppress instinctive desires, he has a will of his own, he chooses between incompatible ends.... (*The Ultimate Foundation of Economic Science*, p. 57)

So, yes, our choices are subjective, and our actions are in no sense determined (defined in advance) by forces inside or outside us. But objective factors to be considered in turning subjective preferences into action dwarf everything else, and we need every tool at our disposal to try to help us improve the odds if we want to survive and thrive, not fail and perish.

> There is within the infinite expanse of what is called the universe or nature a small field in which man's conscious conduct can influence the course of events.... (*The Ultimate Foundation of Economic Science*, p. 11)

> Man is only a tiny speck in the infinite vastness of the universe and that the whole history of mankind is but a fleeting episode in the endless flux of eternity.... (*The Ultimate Foundation of Economic Science*, p. 125)

If we make an accurate estimate of our place in the world and how much works against us in the immediate moment, it is folly to pretend, to ignore reality, to follow our impulses, and hope simply to impose our subjective wishes on the world. The only rational course is to accept the imperative to plan ahead and act sustainably. Mises reminds us that:

> Truth refers to what is or was, not to a state of affairs that is not or was not but would suit the wishes of the truth-seeker better.... (*Theory and History*, p. 298)

> Truth is not the halfway point between two untruths.... (*On the Manipulation of Money and Credit*, p. 88)

> ... The criterion of truth is that it works even if nobody is prepared to acknowledge it.... (*The Ultimate Foundation of Economic Science*, p. 94)

> At least one of the characteristic marks of a true theory is that action based on it succeeds in attaining the expected result. In this sense, truth works while untruth does not work.... (*Theory and History*, p. 123)

> Truth persists and works, even if nobody is left to utter it.... (*Austrian Economics: An Anthology*, p. 76)

This does not mean that anyone can afford to be dogmatic about truth; life is far too complicated for that. As Mises said:

Man can never become omniscient. He can never be absolutely certain that his inquiries were not misled and that what he considers as certain truth is not error. All that man can do is to submit all his theories again and again to the most critical reexamination.... (*Human Action,* p. 68)

Social Cooperation Is a Solution but Also Imposes Its Own Severe Constraints

Perhaps the hardest truths we have to learn are the truths of social cooperation. It is hard to learn them day to day growing up in the context of a family or school or neighborhood. It is even harder when these truths apply to a society as a whole and become more and more abstract for us. It is all too easy for us to rationalize that these often unwelcome truths do not apply to us or do not apply to our country. Why not? What cost is there? Or what cost now and why worry about the future since as economist John Maynard Keynes correctly noted: "In the long run we are all dead." The trouble with this facile thinking is that the result can be utter ruin, and although it may arrive with lags, it can also arrive more quickly than we expect. On the more positive side, if we embrace reality, and its corollaries, social cooperation and civilization, we can achieve more than we ever expected.

Mises notes that:

> What distinguishes civilized man from a barbarian must be acquired by every individual anew.... (*Theory and History*, p. 293)

> Man is born an asocial and antisocial being. The newborn child is a savage. Egoism is his nature. Only the experience of life and the teachings of his parents, his brothers, sisters, play-mates, and later of other people force him to acknowledge the advantages of social cooperation and accordingly to change his behavior. The savage thus turns toward civilization and citizenship.... (*Omnipotent Government*, p. 241)

> What distinguishes man from animals is the insight into the advantages that can be derived from cooperation under the division of labor. Man curbs his innate instinct of aggression in order to cooperate with other human beings. The more he wants to improve his material well-being, the more he must expand the system of the division of labor.... (*Human Action*, pp. 827, 831)

> ...Peaceful cooperation under the principle of the division of labor is a better method to preserve life and to remove felt uneasiness

than indulging in pitiless biological competition for a share in the scarce means of subsistence provided by nature. . . . (*The Ultimate Foundation of Economic Science*, p. 97)

The moral precepts and the laws of the country are means by which men seek to attain
certain ends. Whether or not these ends can
really be attained this way depends on the
laws of the universe. The man-made laws are
suitable if they are fit to attain these ends
and contrary to purpose if they are not. They
are open to examination from the point of
view of their suitableness or unsuitable-
ness. . . . (*Human Action*, pp. 756, 761–62)

That everyone lives and wishes to live primarily for himself does not disturb social
life but promotes it, for the higher fulfill-
ment of the individual's life is possible only
in and through society. . . . (*Socialism*, p. 361)

In social cooperation everyone in serving
his own interests serves the interests of his
fellow men. Driven by the urge to improve
his own conditions, he improves the conditions of other people. The baker does not
hurt those for whom he bakes bread; he
serves them. . . . (*The Ultimate Foundation
of Economic Science*, p. 88)

How do we discover the truths, including the social truths, we need in order to succeed in helping each other and thus in enabling ourselves to realize our individual goals? The greatest tools we have are, first, logic, then experience, and finally an integration of those tools in science.

The Centrality of Logic

Logical thinking and real life are not two separate orbits. Logic is for man the only means to master the problems of reality.... (*Interventionism,* p. 90)

Reason is the main resource of man in his struggle for survival.... (*Omnipotent Government,* p. 121)

It is vain to object that life and reality are not logical. Life and reality are neither logical nor illogical; they are simply given. But logic is the only tool available to man for the comprehension of both.... (*Human Action,* pp. 67–68)

The logical structure of human thought is immutable throughout the whole course of time and is the same for all races, nations, and classes.... (*Epistemological Problems of Economics,* p. 204)

We can speak to each other only because we can appeal to something common to all of us, namely, the logical structure of reason.... (*Omnipotent Government,* p. 143)

Man uses reason in order to choose between the incompatible satisfactions of conflicting desires.... (*Human Action,* pp. 173-74)

Reason is man's particular and characteristic feature. There is no need for praxeology to raise the question whether reason is a suitable tool for the cognition of ultimate and absolute truth. It deals with reason only as far as it enables man to act.... (*Human Action,* p. 177)

Experience Also Counts

Experience is a mental act on the part of thinking and acting men.... (*The Ultimate Foundation of Economic Science,* p. 15)

Experience tells us something we did not know before and could not learn but for having had the experience.... (*The Ultimate Foundation of Economic Science,* p. 18)

New experience can force us to discard or modify inferences we have drawn from previous experience.... (*Epistemological Problems of Economics,* p. 27)

If there were no regularity, nothing could be learned from experience.... (*The Ultimate Foundation of Economic Science*, p. 21)

It would be vain to search for a rule if there were no regularity.... (*The Ultimate Foundation of Economic Science*, p. 22)

Economic Science (Integrating Logic and Experience)

Science is competent to establish what *is*. It can never dictate what ought to be.

In the realm of nature we cannot know anything about final causes, by reference to which events can be explained. But in the field of human actions there is the finality of acting men.... (*Planned Chaos*, p. 30)

Men make choices. They aim at certain ends and they apply means in order to attain the ends sought.... (*Omnipotent Government*, p. 120)

There are no laboratory experiments in human action.... (*Economic Policy*, p. 35)

What matters is not whether a doctrine is new, but whether it is sound.... (*Planning for Freedom*, p. 53); (*Epistemological Problems of Economics*, p. 46)

Science cannot go beyond its own sphere. It must limit itself to the development of our system of knowledge and with its help undertake the logical elaboration of experience.... (*Epistemological Problems of Economics,* p. 201)

Nothing could be more mistaken than the now fashionable attempt to apply the methods and concepts of the natural sciences to the solution of social problems.... (*Omnipotent Government,* p. 120)

What makes natural science possible is the power to experiment; what makes social science possible is the power to grasp or to comprehend the meaning of human action.... (*Money, Method, and the Market Process,* p. 9)

Economic Truths [Laws] May Be Derived From The Praxeological Analysis of the Constraints of Human Action

The following selection is only a small, illustrative sample:

Capital

Nobody ever contended that one could produce without working.... [But] there are no means by which the general standard of living can be raised other than by accelerating the increase of capital as compared with population.... (*Planning for Freedom*, pp. 5–6, 111)

Capital does not reproduce itself.... (*Socialism*, p. 177)

Savings

The only source of the generation of additional capital goods is saving. If all the goods produced are consumed, no new capital comes into being.... (*The Anti-Capitalistic Mentality*, p. 84)

Capital is not a free gift of God or of nature. It is the outcome of a provident restriction of consumption on the part of man. It is created and increased by saving and maintained by the abstention from dissaving.... (*The Anti-Capitalistic Mentality*, p. 84)

The most ingenious technological inventions would be practically useless if the capital goods required for their utilization had not been accumulated by saving.... (*The Anti-Capitalistic Mentality*, p. 39)

We are the lucky heirs of our fathers and forefathers whose saving has accumulated the capital goods with the aid of which we are working today. We favorite children of the age of electricity still derive advantage from the original saving of the primitive fishermen who, in producing the first nets and canoes, devoted a part of their working time to provision for a remoter future. . . . (*Human Action,* p. 489)

Money Supply

If it were really possible to substitute credit expansion (cheap money) for the accumulation of capital goods by saving, there would not be any poverty in the world. . . . (*Planning for Freedom*, p. 190)

Depression is the aftermath of credit expansion. . . . (*Planning for Freedom*, p. 7)

Credit expansion is not a nostrum to make people happy. The boom it engenders must inevitably lead to a debacle and unhappiness. . . . (*Planning for Freedom*, p. 189)

The essence of a credit-expansion boom is not overinvestment, but investment in wrong lines, i.e., malinvestment. . . . (*Human Action,* p. 556)

What is needed for a sound expansion of production is additional capital goods, not money or fiduciary media. The credit boom is built on the sands of banknotes and deposits. It must collapse.... (*Human Action,* pp. 559, 561)

If the credit expansion is not stopped in time, the boom turns into the crack-up boom; the flight into real values begins, and the whole monetary system founders.... (*Human Action,* pp. 559, 562)

The final outcome of the credit expansion is general impoverishment.... (*Human Action,* pp. 562, 564)

If you increase the quantity of money, you bring about the lowering of the purchasing power of the monetary unit.... (*Economic Policy,* p. 66)

The quantity of money available in the whole economy is always sufficient to secure for everybody all that money does and can do.... (*Human Action,* pp. 418, 421)

No nation need fear at any time to have less money than it needs.... (*The Theory of Money and Credit,* pp. 208–09)

The entrepreneurs who approach banks for loans are suffering from shortage of capital;

it is never shortage of money in the proper sense of the word.... (*The Theory of Money and Credit*, p. 349)

Price Control

Mises regarded government policies aimed at increasing the money supply through credit expansion as an important form of indirect price control, in this case control of the all-important rate of interest charged borrowers. But he opposed all price controls, not just monetary ones, on both praxeological and historical grounds:

> Even capital punishment could not make [general] price control work in the days of Emperor Diocletian and the French Revolution.... (*Defense, Control, and Inflation*, pp. 109–10)

> Economics does not say that isolated government interference with the prices of only one commodity or a few commodities is unfair, bad, or unfeasible. It says that such interference produces results contrary to its purpose, that it makes conditions worse, not better, *from the point of view of the government and those backing its interference*.... (*The Theory of Money and Credit*, p. 281)

We first introduced Ludwig von Mises in the introduction of this book in the following terms:

> Ludwig von Mises is generally sympathetic with Hume's approach. Like Hume, he begins with considerable skepticism about traditional philosophical metaphysics, of which he says:
>
> > It is not to be denied that the loftiest theme that human thought can set for itself is reflection on ultimate questions. Whether such reflection can accomplish anything is doubtful. . . . (*Epistemological Problems of Economics,* p. 49)

Mises, however, does much more than simply agree with Hume. He clarifies many points. For example, he explains that, yes, all our choices are individual and thus subjective. But we do not make those choices in a world of our own choosing, however much we might like to deny this. We must face the reality of the physical and social worlds in which we live, and this reality imposes on us many objective rules. If we want to survive, we must eat, and if we want to eat, we must gather food, and so forth. By using our logic, and learning from experience, we can develop a system of objective rules that will enable us to consider the long term as well as the short term and to work together to meet our needs and even realize many of our desires. If we are unable to rein in our subjective desires in order to conform them to physical reality and find common ground with others, we will eventually perish.

In effect, then, Mises is asking us to overcome the clashes of self-interest in the immediate social or political context, and instead focus on the long term and on the choice of policies and actions that are truly sustainable. Sustainability is his central theme. Will the human race demonstrate sufficiently mature judgment to heed this message and work together toward long-term shared goals, or will we instead commit collective suicide?

Mises disciple, economic writer Henry Hazlitt (1894–1993), took both David Hume's ideas and those of Mises and developed them into a complete moral philosophy under the name Cooperatism (or Mutualism) in his book, *The Foundations of Morality*. The approach is broadly utilitarian, but rule-utilitarian, and also what Hazlitt would have called classically liberal but which we now more commonly refer to as libertarian. The basic idea* is that we all need each other; no one can stand alone. But in order to foster the right kind of cooperation, the place to start is with an ideal

---

* The description of Hazlitt's cooperatism contains material published in Hunter Lewis, *A Question of Values* (San Francisco: Harper Collins, 1990) under the alternative name of reciprocalism.

of independence, of each economic player taking personal responsibility for himself or herself, doing his or her part, standing as far as possible on his or her own feet, not being an unnecessary burden on others, and thereby earning not only self-respect and good will, but also the communal assistance of others. Among the problems with the family model writ larger and larger in the modern state, is that it feeds the grandiosity of parental leaders, bestows far too much power (with all its temptations) on them, and infantilizes everyone else.

Moreover, we are told, a philosophy of independence, personal responsibility, and reciprocal cooperation makes us happier. As a side note on this point, naturalist and philosopher Alexander Skutch (1904–2004) has reminded us that

> if we remember that the stranger of whom we ask a direction owes nothing to us, his courteous response will be more appreciated and will lighten our steps if the journey is long. If we never expect anything of anybody, we shall … be more grateful for everything that is done for us.[139]

Hazlitt's cooperatism further teaches that:

- We serve ourselves best by serving others, for example by producing the finest goods we can make and honestly exchanging them for those of others;

- Exchanging is healthier than giving, because neither giving nor taking are healthy if isolated from each other;*
- Competition is healthy if channeled into constructive projects for the betterment of humanity;
- Free economic markets are the right place for competition;
- Free global markets should be fostered and will reduce or someday even extinguish war;
- Pluralism is better than centralized, hierarchical leadership;
- Change should be welcomed, not resisted as socially destabilizing;
- Competing entrepreneurs, operating in free markets, are the essential agents of constructive change, economic growth and progress;
- Knowledge and discovery are critical to successful entrepreneurship;
- People should not be protected from the consequences of their own choices or actions;
- Whenever people are protected from their own errors, mistakes accumulate instead of being

---

* This is evidently quite an old idea, since the ancient Indo-European root for the modern English word "giving" seems to have meant either giving or taking or both giving and taking, which suggests that early humans viewed these actions as being so closely related that a single word sufficed for both.

liquidated, and economic growth and social improvements grind to a halt;

- Trust, honesty, decency, self-discipline, thrift, saving, and patience (what in the nineteenth century was called "character"), will eventually lead us, through the power of compounding our capital, out of poverty and deprivation.

Conclusion

As interesting and important as Hazlitt's work is in elaborating on Hume and Mises, it is important to reiterate that Mises's essential insight, independent of any rules derived from it, is that acting human beings face objective, not subjective choices. Our choices are necessarily objective, because we live in the real world, not the world of our dreams, and if we want to get anywhere we must get in step with reality. As much as we might regret it, reality will never get in step with us.

Chapter 16
Eudora Welty[*]
(1909–2001)

NOVELIST, SHORT STORY writer, and photographer Eudora Welty possessed acutely developed powers of seeing and hearing. To illustrate this, consider how she begins a brief memoir of her early life in Jackson, Mississippi. She focuses on sounds, especially the sounds of her parents:

> I'd listen toward the hall: Daddy upstairs was shaving in the bathroom and Mother downstairs was frying the bacon. They would begin whistling back and forth to each other

---

[*] This chapter includes material pubished in Hunter Lewis, *A Question of Values* (San Francisco: Harper Collins, 1990).

up and down the stairwell. My father would
whistle his phrase, my mother would try to
whistle, then hum hers back. It was their duet
[from] "The Merry Widow." . . . Their song
almost floated with laughter: how different
from the [Victrola] record, which growled.[140]

Later, when Eudora was a young woman, her powers
of observation lead her to "make pictures with a cam-
era." Both in her photographs of a deeply impoverished
Mississippi during the Depression and in her more celebrated fiction, Welty's unblinking but warmly compassionate gaze seemed to penetrate into the very "mind,
heart, and skin" of her subjects.

Where does such heightened sense experience, heightened hearing and seeing, take us in our personal philosophy or ethics? Like French philosopher Michel de
Montaigne, treated earlier, Miss Welty is reluctant to
say; indeed, it might be said to be contrary to her values
to comment directly. After all, she suggests, the point of
hearing and seeing is to hear and see for yourself.

If you want to know what a fiction writer and photographer in Mississippi has heard and seen, you should
read her fiction or look at her photographs, then make
up your own mind about what it means for you. The
point of art is to broaden the reader/viewer/listener's
sense experience, put people and things in a different,
perhaps a more revealing or telling, perspective, not to
serve up ready-made answers.

This might seem to be an uncompromising attitude, but it is tempered by Miss Welty's warmth, calm, and graciousness. She lived her entire life in the same house on the tree-lined street in Jackson, first caring for her mother, then living alone. The house is now a museum and well worth visiting. But she was also a woman of the world.

Her friend Henry Miller, author of novels that were initially banned in the United States and Britain and only legal in France, came to Jackson for a three night visit. He was taken out to dinner each night and in a subsequent letter expressed surprise that Jackson had three such good restaurants. Miss Welty was amused, since it had actually been the same restaurant, which Miller had evidently missed in a haze of alcohol. She also politely and affectionately declined his offer to help her increase her income by putting her in touch with a publisher of pornography, an offer that she did not share with her mother, but nevertheless rather appreciated.

As the years passed, the wise, compassionate, observant, and often funny stories poured forth and found a wide audience. Newspaper interviewers and PhD candidates appeared at her door, often with no invitation or advance notice, and were usually taken in for some homemade baked goods and a friendly chat. If these interviewers were unhurried, listened intently, and enjoyed good conversation, they had much to learn from the experience.

Chapter 17

Edna Lewis

(1916–2006)

EDNA LEWIS ROSE from humble origins, grandaughter of an enslaved plantation worker, and almost single-handedly revived fine Southern cooking. Thanks to her, this style of food is not only increasingly popular in America, but also admired around the world. Those who love this sometimes simple but often complicated and sophisticated food and regard it as one of the world's great cuisines owe a lot to the woman who has been referred to as the "*Grande Dame* of Southern cooking" and "the South's answer to Julia Child."

The famous American chef James Beard said, "Edna Lewis makes me want to go right into the kitchen and start cooking." That is how many people feel about her. The US government honored her achievement with a commemorative postal stamp acknowledging her place among the greatest American chefs. The stamp is a head shot, so you don't see her tall, lithe body, often clothed in African fabrics, or her dignified and way of moving and talking. "You couldn't walk down the street without people stopping [her]: 'You're so beautiful I want to paint you, photograph you,'" reports Scott Peacock, former executive chef of Watershed Restaurant in Decatur, Georgia, a famous Southern chef himself, and co-author of her last book.

Lewis also had a gift for living and for friendship. She counted friends among the poorest and the richest of Americans. She listened carefully and thoughtfully to everyone's concerns and offered advice that was always grounded in common sense but that nevertheless came straight from the heart. No wonder so many people loved her. And she knew how to live. Everything she touched came alive with inspiration and pleasure, even simple tasks such as selecting food or preparing a meal.

Edna Lewis was born on April 13, 1916, in Freetown, Virginia, a small town established and named by three former slaves, including her grandfather Chester Lewis. She was one of eight children. The families in Freetown were largely self-sufficient, foraging or raising their own food and meat, with a few purchases from a nearby general store. Water was pumped by hand from the ground, and heat in the winter was by wood fire or old Franklin Stove.

Of life in Freetown, Lewis said: "If someone borrowed one cup of sugar, they would return two. If someone fell ill, the neighbors would go in and milk the cows, feed the chickens, clean the house, cook the food and come and sit with whoever was sick. I guess rural life conditioned people to cooperate with their neighbors."

What the family ate changed with the seasons. Lewis learned to cook (on a wood stove) by watching and imitating the other women of the family. Where tools were lacking, the cooks improvised. For example, they could not afford measuring spoons, so they measured homemade baking powder on coins.

After leaving Freetown at age 16 to earn money for the family, Lewis moved to Washington, DC and then to New York. Jobs included ironing (she did not really know how to iron and lost that job within hours), domestic work, and seamstress. After making dresses for celebrities such as Marilyn Monroe, she became the window "dresser" at Bonwit Teller, a fashionable department store, an important and well-paid job, but in 1948 left to become chef and partner at Café Nicholson, a new restaurant owned by a friend, a wealthy and well-connected New York Bohemian named John Nicholson. Customers included Paul Robeson, Tennessee Williams, Gore Vidal, Truman Capote, William Faulkner, Richard Avedon, Marlene Dietrich, Diana

Vreeland, Howard Hughes, Eleanor Roosevelt, and Gloria Vanderbilt, among many other celebrities.

Café Nicholson became a Manhattan "in" spot thanks to Lewis's cooking and charm. The *New York Times* notes that "restaurant critic Clementine Paddleford reviewed the restaurant in 1951 in the *New York Herald Tribune*, calling the soufflé 'light as a dandelion seed in a wind' and noting a sense of pride in the chef: 'We saw Edna peering in from the kitchen, just to see the effect on the guests and hear the echoes of praise.'" In reading this, we must keep in mind that women chefs were rare enough at that time, black women chefs unheard of.

In 1954, Lewis left the Café, partly at the request of her husband Steve Kingston, a Communist Party member and organizer, who objected to her feeding "the capitalists." Together they started a pheasant farm in New Jersey that failed. Eventually Lewis became chef at Gage and Tollner, a famous restaurant in Brooklyn she put back on the map as a fashionable stop for wealthy New Yorkers. She also worked as a volunteer at the American Museum of American History, which she loved. In 1972, she published her first cookbook, *The Edna Lewis Cookbook*, which was immediately praised by both James Beard and M. K. F. Fisher, the two best-known food writers of the day. It was followed in 1976 by a second book, *The Taste of Country Cooking*, then in 1988 *In Pursuit of Flavor*, and in 2003, *The Gift of Southern Cooking*, with her student and friend Scott Peacock.

The Edna Lewis Cookbook includes some not Southern recipes but already introduces the idea of local ingredients and seasonal focus. *The Taste of Country Cooking* and *The Gift of Southern Cooking* are both considered high points of southern food history.

In 1990, Ms. Lewis received the Lifetime Achievement Award of IACP (International Assoc. of Culinary Professionals) and in 1995 the James Beard Foundation's Living Legend Award (their first such award.) In her last years, she lived with Mr. Peacock in Atlanta and died, aged 89, in 2006.

Part Five

Conclusion

Chapter 18

Why Morals Are Not Just Subjective

WHAT, IF ANYTHING, can be learned from the accumulated thinking of moral philosophers, if only a very small and necessarily incomplete sample drawn for reasons of space from Western rather than world history, individuals whose lives as well as thought seem to fit them for the term "secular saint," along with others who were not philosophers in the usual sense, but whose life and thought represented a beacon light for others?

Even what has been covered in this book, with all its important omissions, especially of non-Western and contemporary moral philosophers, cannot be summarized in a short, concluding chapter. But here are a few concluding thoughts.

Nobody can exist without goals. Human beings are just made that way. Our goals are as necessary for us as food, water, and shelter, or even more necessary. As von Mises said, we are beings made for action, and to act we must have a direction in which to act.

We always choose our goals through the mental means we have at our disposal, which means a combination of emotion, intuition (quite different from emotion), sense experience (with its focus on facts), and logic. No one of these four is dominant, and they continually interact and influence each other.

If we can't find our goals anywhere else, we will find them in nihilism and self-destruction. Put simply, we would rather destroy ourselves and others than face a life without a shred of even contingent purpose or meaning.

Let those who propose that most work be done by robots take note. The human species is not built for retirement at a young age, and unoccupied, aimless young people will strike back in ways that society will not like.

Each of us chooses his or her goals, nobody else can choose them for us. On the other hand, we do not really have a lot of goals. Most of our supposed goals are just means to some other end. Perhaps we have the goal of getting a good job. But it is not ultimately the job we want so much as what comes along with a good job, including learning, stimulation, social life, money, and, not least, feeling independent, feeling good about ourselves, making a contribution to society, and having a reason to get up each morning. Whatever goals we choose, whether they really are goals or rather means to further ends, if we do not understand that life has its rules or if we refuse to observe those rules, we cannot expect to get very far.

Life is not a game, but like a game it has rules. Those rules are quite objective because they reflect both physical and social realities. The rules are not spelled out for us. Part of the challenge is that the rules can be extremely complicated, not easily codified apart from laws, and they also change from time to time as reality changes.

The concept of having generally applicable rules of action is crucial, as David Hume noted. We not only need them to deal with the complexity of life, which would otherwise be overwhelming. We also need them because just as any choice has at least two sides, any specific action is likely to have at least a double edge, or at a minimum, bring along some unintended consequences.

Not only is it often challenging to sort out the best path toward any single (seemingly meritorious) goal, but most of the time we simultaneously have to balance the claims of numerous meritorious goals, all of which may be conflicting to a degree at a given moment. We cannot tell our children how to navigate in a maze of not-yet-defined, much less, imagined situations. But we can give them some rules that will help them sort out the choices when the time comes.

Each one of us has a choice not only about goals, but also about whether we want to try to harmonize ourselves with reality and increase our chances of attaining our objectives by following rules, or whether we do not wish to do so. We often choose to turn our eyes away from reality. As the 19th-century romantic Italian poet Leopardi wrote:

> No one understands the human heart at all who does not understand how vast is its capacity for illusions, even when these are contrary to its interests, or how often it loves the very things that are obviously harmful to it.[141]

Leopardi is correct. He might also have added that there is no shortage of people who will try to encourage us in our illusions. They might do so for many reasons. They may not want to face reality themselves. Or they may be deliberately deceiving us in order to persuade us to do something they want us to do, such as vote for them, or buy something or borrow money because it helps their business. Moreover there is no shortage of "experts" who for a payment will argue on behalf of the deceivers.

This is unfortunately a pitfall of life. It is indeed confusing to have so many false advisers and prophets to contend with. But if we choose for whatever reason to deceive ourselves, to embrace nonsense, if we fail at least to try to discover and try to follow the rules of reality, we must not expect to have much chance of achieving our subjectively chosen goals.

If we discover and follow the rules of life as it really is, not as we would wish it were, we have the enormous advantage that the world will stand less in our way and other people are more likely to help us. Without their help, we are almost always doomed to frustration and failure, which even romantic poets rarely espouse as their stated goal.

Here is a concrete example. Assume that you have been diagnosed with pancreatic cancer. This conflicts with your subjective goal of staying alive. How will you react? Will you focus exclusively on your subjective goal and the feelings that go with that? If so, you might deny the diagnosis as too painful to contemplate. Or you might turn your case over to the nearest oncologist and tell yourself that this parental figure will care for and heal you. Or you might try to deal as squarely with reality and the rules of life as you possibly can.

If you adopt the second point of view, you will take advantage of the internet and appraise the factual information on it as coolly, objectively, and logically as you possibly can. This will not be easy. How can it be easy to face death?

You will learn that your chances of surviving for five years with conventional chemotherapy or radiation are only about 6%, that these treatments are excruciating, and that they may actually hasten death by killing off the weaker cancer cells and leaving the cancer stem cells, which then may become much more aggressive and metastatic. You will acknowledge that oncologists work in a system that is closely restricted by government regulation and the threat of legal liability and also have certain financial incentives. For example, oncologists are legally allowed to profit from the sale of chemotherapy drugs while other doctors are not allowed to profit from the sale of drugs.

Even if an oncologist is devoted to patients and gives no weight to financial incentive and little to legal liability, regulation still governs, and none of these things has anything to do with your case or your needs, so it would be unrealistic to expect the doctor to decide entirely based on what is best for you. Moreover, in the age of specialists, you will not just be dealing with one doctor, but with several, along with interlocking medical, insurance, and government bureaucracies. You might wish all of this were otherwise, but your wishes are not reality.

You can then use this information as a starting point in the exploration of treatments, medical or spiritual, that might postpone death or at least improve the quality of what time remains. Either way, you would be getting as closely in accord with reality as you possibly can, which is likely to give you the best possible outcome under the circumstances. The point of this rather grim example is that neither the physical world nor most other people care what you want or feel, and it is up to you to get as much as you can in harmony with reality, because reality will not try to get in harmony with you.

Lest this sound like it is all about the need for a coolly logical appraisal of a situation, it is not. Once the fact-gathering and logical appraisal is completed, and a plan developed, the individual will still need to summon up the emotional reserves needed to act on the plan. The patient will in particular need to fall back on the critical emotional virtues of courage and of acceptance, among others. No human being is all about fact or logic. All the mental modes and virtues have to work together in tandem.

Society in past times provided individuals with a lot of help in discovering and following the rules that would allow them to make the best peace they could with reality. For some reason, we now just throw even young people in the deep end of the pool with very little instruction or help.

We also have to keep in mind that the rules are always imperfect; at best they are based on probabilities, not certainties. But, even so, reality, and the probalistic rules developed to cope with reality, are ignored at our peril.

To the degree that the rules are important enough to become codified in law, they can also become mind-numbingly complex. There are so many laws now, and so many written in dense tangles of words only decipherable by a lawyer, or so subject to subjective interpretation, that the average person should hope to remain unnoticed, since he or she is otherwise left at the mercy of government officials who may or may not prosecute unintentional violations, even if the statute requires intentionality.

As everyone acknowledges, law is supposed to cover only the basics of human behavior. Beyond law, there are all the personal decisions and behaviors that fall under the headings of "character" or "common sense." These are not empty, specious concepts, however unfashionable and however uncommon character and common sense have become.

It is permissible at the present time to say approvingly that someone has a high "emotional IQ." People with a high "emotional IQ" do not simply understand better what other people are feeling or are likely to feel under particular circumstances. They also understand that life has rules, accept them, and follow them both for moral and practical reasons. They appreciate harmony and the role harmony can play in helping them achieve their objectives as well in making life much more pleasurable for everyone.

There are those who regard life as a game in which they can set their own rules. It may seem to work for a time. But usually the more it seems to work, the harder the eventual fall. Hitler provides a prime example, but examples are legion.

Hitler also reminds us that tribalism has become deadly for human beings. Throughout history, it has been convenient for tribal leaders to create tribal unity by re-directing bad feelings and conflicts outside onto others. Occasionally this is done by scapegoating some poor individual or individuals within the tribe (e.g. German Jews), but more often by promoting enmity or conflict with other tribes, or by seeking to prey on other tribes.

This behavior has always been a stain on the human race. It has also prevented the kind of global cooperation needed to pull everyone out of poverty. It ensured that most people's lives would be "brutal, nasty, and short," as philosopher Thomas Hobbes put it. It is quite clear that, as bad as it was in the past, tribalism is now even more at odds with the realities of the world, with its weapons of mass destruction. It is an objective fact that tribal politics are disastrous, even though world leaders such as Vladimir Putin, the Iranian Mullahs, the Chinese Politburo leaders, and to a much lesser degree American, Japanese, and European leaders routinely exploit it to maintain themselves in power.

Tribal leaders have also relied in the past on outside conflict to distract their followers from their own intra-tribe predation and parasitism. In the modern age, the most common form this corruption takes is crony capitalism, in which organized special interests of all kinds ally themselves with government officials in order to win government favors or dispensation from market rules, especially in the form of lucrative economic monopolies. Government officials in turn receive campaign contributions and other benefits in addition to lucrative jobs when they return to the private sector or when they rotate back and forth between public and private jobs.

Competitive markets are tough regulators. Why work hard at keeping quality up and prices down and face the ever-present risk of bankruptcy because of poor performance, when all you have to do is buy off government officials and escape market discipline? Although Big Business is a major player in this game of buying government, so are all the Bigs: Big Labor, Big Law, Big Medicine, even Big Education, among others.

18th-century reformers such as Adam Smith argued that traditional tribal forms of government, in which political leaders have ultimate control over the economy as well as all other aspects of society, cannot help but lead to the corruption of crony capitalism. Anytime businessmen in the same industry meet together, with themselves or especially with government officials, some conspiracy against the public will be hatched.

In this view, the only way to control crony capitalism is to forbid governments to involve themselves in economic management, especially management of the market price-setting system. Government would continue to establish universal laws governing the economy, which would be applicable to everyone and would continue to maintain the courts. But day-to-day control of the economy by regulators empowered to make their own decisions would not be allowed.

20th-century progressives agreed that crony capitalist corruption is an immense problem, but thought that expanding rather than restricting the power of government, along with finding more virtuous people to serve in public office, would better address the problem. These issues remain highly contentious and unresolved. So long as they remain unresolved, crony capitalism will continue to be the dominant economic system throughout the world, will continue to get worse rather than better, will thwart efforts to create lasting forms of global economic cooperation, and will continue to impoverish billions of people while benefiting a relatively few already rich individuals. This is a very high price to pay for clinging to primitive tribal thinking and outmoded tribal forms of social organization that invite corruption and misuse of political power.

The ancient Roman poet Horace and others said that "justice often follows with a limp." This means that even conscious, much less unconscious, wrongdoing may seem to be rewarded in the short term. But one of the rules of life is that we must look to the long term as well as the short term, notwithstanding economist John Maynard Keynes jibe that "in the long run we are all dead."

A wit replied to Keynes that this was the only true thing he ever said. But, true or not, we have to act on the assumption that there is a tomorrow, if not always for us, then most of the time for us, and if not for us, then for our loved ones or the human race, and we need to act responsibly and sustainably, in order to achieve what we can and to prevent tomorrow from being horrific.

Being human, we are always faced with unexpected or disguised temptations. As central as the concept of sustainability is from an ethical point of view, it, like any other concept, can be distorted and misused. An article in the *DailyCaller.com*, a self-described conservative website, complained in 2015 that politically "progressive" professors were trying to indoctrinate college students by flying the sustainability banner above ideas that were demonstrably unsustainable, such as huge government deficit spending.

The "progressive" professors might in turn make the same claim about some "conservative" ideas, such as low taxation. The truth is that huge government deficit spending is indeed unsustainable, whether driven by too much spending or low taxation or both.

In his book, *Moral Foundations*, the ornithologist, naturalist, and philosopher Alexander Skutch (1904–2004) provided a shrewd appraisal of the concept of genuine sustainability:

> People . . . might tell us that . . . morality . . .
> is not lying, not stealing, not killing, not

coveting, not cheating, [not] . . . injuring one's neighbor. If asked what common feature unites all these interdicted activities, they would find it difficult to answer. They might say that all these forbidden activities cause people pain. . . . This is true enough, but . . . competition in trade or the professions brings much loss and sorrow to those who fail in it; . . . the punishment of children makes them unhappy; and the practice of medicine and dentistry are abundant sources of pain even to those who ultimately benefit. . . . The common feature which unites the activities most consistently forbidden by the moral codes of civilized peoples is that by their very nature they cannot be both habitual and enduring, because they tend to destroy the conditions which make them possible.

As Skutch suggests, sustainability is the essence of both maturity and morality. It is also the foundation for human happiness. As we may recall from earlier in this book, the ancient Greek philosopher Epicurus taught that:

The . . . chief good is care in avoiding undesired consequences. Such prudence is more precious than philosophy itself, for all the other virtues spring from it. It teaches that

it is impossible to live pleasurably without
also living prudently, honestly, and justly;
[nor is it possible to lead a life of prudence,
honor, and justice] and not live pleasantly.
For the virtues are closely associated with
the pleasant life, and the pleasant life cannot be separated from them.

Most discussions of ethics present us with conflicting choices. For example, we can be egoistic or altruistic. We can put ourselves first or we can put others first.
These conflicts are often very real in the short term.
But when we take a longer- term view, informed by
the principle of sustainability, the conflict usually vanishes, as Henry Hazlitt noted in his book, *The Foundations of Morality*.

As everyone knows, we cannot achieve our personal
goals without the help of others. This means that, for all
of us, the principal means to where we want to go is a
system of harmonious social cooperation. Cooperation
may be a means, but it is such an important means that,
for all practical purposes, it becomes a common shared
goal. If I have to sacrifice some of my preferences to
achieve it, that is hardly a sacrifice at all, because I will
get back so much more than I sacrifice.

The idea that ethics are objective, and therefore universal, because subjective goals must be tempered by
a very objective physical and social reality, is a crucial
philosophical insight. So are the ideas of the primacy

of rules and of probability versus certainty, the latter being beyond our reach in this life. So are the ideas of long-term thinking versus short term and the importance of sustainability and cooperation in everything we do. Sustainability and cooperation are the essence of morality. Together with key facts, such as the unsustainability and destruction of cooperation embodied in tribalism and crony capitalism, they represent a beginning of wisdom that, if acted on, will carry us a long way toward a better life.

Endnotes

1. A. J. Ayer, *Language, Truth, and Logic* (New York: Dover Publications, 1952), 119.

2. Bertrand Russell, *Religion and Science* (New York: Oxford University Press, 1961) 238.

3. C. L. Stevenson, "The Emotive Meaning of Ethical Terms" *Mind* (1937): 20.

4. Bertrand Russell, *Fact and Fiction* (London: Allen & Unwin, 1961), 46.

5. Derek Parfit, *Reasons & Persons* (New York: Oxford University Press, 1985), 281.

6. Ibid., 454.

7. Ibid., 451.

8. Ibid., 452.

9. John Rawls, *A Theory of Justice* (Cambridge, Mass: Belknap Press of Harvard University, 1971) 62.

10. Harvard University Press, Loeb Edition, 1928, PD

11. For more such quotations from Erasmus's works, see the excellent chapter on Erasmus in Jim Powell's *The Triumph of Reason*, which is available on the Cato

Institute website, and also Laurence M. Vance's article Erasmus on the Evils of War, lewrockwell.com, Nov 11, 2013.

12. Michel de Montaigne, *Essays*, 1588; from "On Three Kinds of Relationships."

13. Ibid; from "On Three Kinds of Relationships."

14. Ibid; from "On Three Kinds of Relationships."

15. Ibid; from "On Physiognomy."

16. Ibid., from "On Physiognomy."

17. Ibid., from "On Experience."

18. Peter Gay, *The Enlightenment: An Interpretation* (New York: Alfred A. Knopf, 1969), 288.

19. Montaigne, op. cit., from "On Democritus and Heraclitus."

20. Ibid., from "On Books."

21. Ibid., from "On Experience."

22. Ibid., from "On Cruelty."

23. Ibid., from "On the Power of the Imagination."

24. Ibid., from "On Repentance."

25. Ibid., from "On the Education of Children."

26. Ibid., from "On Presumption."

27. Ibid., from "On Repentance."

28. Ibid., from "Apology for Raimond Sebond."

29. Ibid., from "That It Is Folly to Measure Truth and Error by Our Own Capacity."

30. Ibid., from "On Experience."

31. Ibid., from "On Books."

32. Ibid., from "On Experience."

33. Ibid., from "On Experience."

34. Ibid., from "On the Education of Children."

35. Ibid., from "On the Education of Children."

36. Ibid., from "Apology for Raimond Sebond."

37. Ibid., from "On Experience."

38. Ibid., from "On Repentance."

39. Ibid., from "On Experience."

40. Ibid., from "On Experience."

41. Ibid., from "On Experience."

42. Ibid., from "On Experience."

43. Gay, op. cit. (Voltaire to Comte de Tresson, August 21, 1746, Correspondence, XV. 119–20X).

44. Montaigne, op. cit., from "On Three Kinds of Relationships."

45. Ibid., from "On Experience."

46. Ibid., from "On Experience."

47. Ibid., from "On Three Kinds of Relationships."

48. Ibid., from "On Three Kinds of Relationships."

49. Ibid., from "On Three Kinds of Relationships."

50. Ibid., from "On Friendship."

51. Ibid., from "On Cannibals."

52. Ibid., from "On the Art of Conversation."

53. Ibid., from "On Presumption."

54. Ibid., from "On Repentance."

55. Ibid., from "On the Control of the Will."

56. Ibid., from "On Three Kinds of Relationships."

57. Ibid., from "On Three Kinds of Relationships."

58. Ibid., from "On Experience."

59. Ibid., from "On Experience."

60. Ibid., from "On the Education of Children."

61. Ibid., from "On Liars."

62. Ibid., from "On the Education of Children."

63. Ibid., from "On Experience."

64. Ibid., from "On the Education of Children."

65. Ibid., from "On Repentance."

66. Ibid., from "On Democritus and Heraclitus."

67. Ibid., from "On Three Kinds of Relationships."

68. Ibid., from "On Experience."

69. Ibid., from "On Experience."

70. Ibid., from "On Experience."

71. Ibid., from "On Experience."

72. Ibid., from "On the Education of Children."

73. Ibid., from "On the Education of Children."

74. Ibid., from "On the Education of Children."

75. Ibid., from "On the Education of Children."

76. Ibid., from "On Friendship."

77. Ibid., from "On the Education of Children."

78. Ibid., from "On the Power of Imagination."

79. Ibid., from "On Cruelty."

80. Ibid., from "On Experience."

81. Ibid., from "On Presumption."

82. Ibid., from "On Experience."

83. Ibid., from "On Physiognomy."

84. Ibid., from "On Physiognomy."

85. Ibid., from "On Experience."

86. Bertrand Russell, *History of Western Philosophy* (New York: Simon & Schuster, 1945), 516.

87. Montaigne, op. cit., from "On Repentance."

88. Paul Edwards, ed., *Encyclopedia of Philosophy* (New York: Macmillan Publishing and The Free Press, 1967), 332.

89. Joseph Alsop, *The Washington Post* (February 12, 1985): A–21.

90. Montaigne, op. cit., from "On Cruelty."

91. Lawrence Durrell, "The Black Book," quoted in *The Big Supposer: A Dialogue with Marc Alyn* (New York: Grove Press, 1974), 25.

92. Lawrence Durrell, *Prospero's Cell* (New York: Curtis Brown, 1960), 11, 23, 76, 81.

93. Durrell, *The Big Supposer*, op. cit., 53–55.

94. Harold Acton, *More Memoirs of an Esthete* (London: Methuen & Co., 1970), Vol. 2, 54.

95. Ibid., p. 259–61.

96. *W Magazine* (1983).

97. Ibid., July 28, 1986, 42.

98. C. P. Cavafy, *Collected Poems*, trans. Keeley and Sherrard (Princeton: Princeton University Press, 1975), 55.

99. Tennessee Williams, *Memoirs of Tennessee Williams* (New York: Doubleday, 1975), 75.

100. Ibid., 95–96.

101. *Playboy* interview, 108.

102. Williams, op. cit., 247.

103. Ibid., 230.

104. John Kenneth Galbraith, *The Age of Uncertainty* (Boston: Houghton Mifflin Co., 1977), 13.

105. *Essay on the Nature of Commerce on General*, written in French in 1730s (1755).

106. Anne-Robert-Jacques Turgot, *Reflections on The Formation and The Distribution of Wealth* (1770).

107. David Hume, *Essays, Moral and Political* (1748).

108. François Quesnay, Tableau économique (1758).

109. Joseph Schumpeter, *History of Economic Analysis* (Oxford: Oxford University Press, 1954), 184.

110. *Journal of Libertarian Studies* (1990).

111. David Gordon, http://www.mises.org (September 21, 2009).

112. Hunter Lewis, ed., *The Essence of Adam Smith's Wealth of Nations* (Mt. Jackson, VA: Axios Press, 2011), 106.

113. Ibid., 342–343.

114. Ibid., 338.

115. Ibid., 327.

116. Ibid., 107.

117. Ibid., 133.

118. Ibid., 410.

119. Hunter Lewis, *Are The Rich Necessary? Great Economic Arguments and How They Reflect Our Personal Values, Updated & Expanded Edition*, (Mt. Jackson, VA: Axios Press, 2009), 310–311.

120. Lecture in 1775, quoted in Dugald Stewart, *Account of the Life and Writings of Adam Smith LLD*, Section IV, 25.

121. Lewis, ed., *The Essence of Adam Smith's Wealth of Nations*, 316.

122. Adam Smith, *The Theory of Moral Sentiments* (1759), Part IV, chapter 1, 184, para 10.

123. Henry Hazlitt, *The Conquest of Poverty*, (Irvington-on-Hudson, NY: Foundation for Economic Education, 1994), 51.

124. Arthur Okun, *Fortune* (November 1975): 199.

125. Lewis, ed., *The Essence of Adam Smith's Wealth of Nations*, 177.

126. Ibid., 245.

127. Ludwig von Mises, *Human Action: A Treatise on Economics*, (Chicago: Henry Regnery Co., 1966), 422.

128. Lewis, ed., *The Essence of Adam Smith*, 245.

129. Ibid., 273.

130. P. J. O'Rourke, *On the Wealth of Nations: Books that Changed the World* (New York: Atlantic Monthly Press, 2006).

131. Karl Marx, Friedrich Engels, *Critique of the Gotha Program* (1875).

132. "My Early Beliefs," *Keynes, Two Memoirs* (London: Rupert Hart-Davis, 1949).

133. David C. Somervell, *English Thought in the 19th Century* (New York: David McKay Co., 1965), 42.

134. Durant, *Age of Napoleon*, op. cit., 406.

135. Oliver A. Johnson, ed., *Ethics* (New York: Holt Rinehart & Winston, 1984).

136. Russell, Bertrand. *A History of Western Philosophy* (New York: Simon & Schuster, 1945).

137. Hunter Lewis ed., *The Essence of Jane Addams's Twenty Years at Hull House*, (Mt. Jackson, VA: Axios Press, 2012), 43.

138. Ibid, 46.

139. Alexander Skutch, *Life Ascending* (Austin: University of Texas Press, 1985), 218.

140. "Whistling," Eudora Welty, *One Writer's Beginnings* (Cambridge, Mass.: G. K. Hall, 1984) frontispiece.

141. Review by John Gray of newly published *Notebooks of Leopardi* in New Statesman, 9/26/13

Index

A

Acton, Harold
  on aestheticism 137–138
Adages (Erasmus) 93,
  96–97
Addams, Jane 27, 339–355
  Goosie and 351
  Hull House and 339,
    343–345, 349–350,
    353
    Woman's Club 345,
    348
  mother wetting herself
    story 350–351
  Nobel Peace Prize 340
aesthete, the 136–138
afterlife, the 71, 166–169
Alexander the Great 21, 60

Alsop, Joseph
  on high sense experience
    129–130
animal rights 332, 335
*Anti-Capitalistic Mental-
  ity, The* (Mises) 365,
  376–377
Apology, The (Plato) 36,
  39, 40, 45
arête 48
Are the Rich Necessary?
  (Lewis) 279, 287
Aristotle 23, 47–61
  as empiricist 50–52
  biography of 60–61
  common sense of 52–53
  on happiness 20, 47–48